EVANGELISM
AND
YOUR CHURCH

By

C. JOHN MILLER

Presbyterian and Reformed Publishing Co.
Phillipsburg, New Jersey 08865
1980

Unless otherwise noted, Scripture citations are either from the author's own translation or from the Authorized Version.

To Rose Marie and Keren

    for the price you paid for this book

    and

To the heavenly Father

    for the Price You paid for our salvation

    John 3:16

Acknowledgments

For the contents of this work I owe a debt to more people than I can remember. But I especially acknowledge how much I have learned from my colleagues at Westminster Theological Seminary and the officers and people of New Life Presbyterian Church. It is also through the support and encouragement of Ben Wilkinson and Charles Howell of Presbyterian Evangelistic Fellowship that the book came to completion. Finally, full credit must be given to Susan Lutz for her major role in the production of this little volume. Whatever there is of brevity, clarity and simplicity in this study reflects her handiwork. For myself I can take full credit for any of the weaknesses which remain. For the missionary vision which led to this book I give the glory to God who gave it to me through Jesus Christ.

Contents

Contents

Foreword

Because of the example set in his own life and ministry, my good friend, Jack Miller, can get away with writing this hard-hitting (but compassionate) book. Most others couldn't. As pastor of the New Life (Orthodox) Presbyterian Church of Jenkintown, Pa., and teacher of Evangelism at Westminster Theological Seminary, Dr. Miller has had ample opportunity not only to reflect upon the current state of evangelism in local churches in the light of biblical truth, but also to do something about the problems he has uncovered and to teach others how to do so too. Jack has engaged in evangelism both in America and overseas. Out of that background, he writes.

Jack Miller is a Calvinist; that fact becomes clear from page one. He is concerned about the lack of evangelism by Bible-believing Reformed Churches of which he has been a part. This concern, coupled with practical suggestions hammered out of biblical exegesis, permeates the book. In his analysis he treats both misunderstandings and misapplications of doctrine, as well as plainly sinful lethargy at the root of the problem. He addresses himself squarely to these issues. Probably not all of his Reformed brethren would agree with everything in his analysis. That really doesn't matter so long as they avail themselves of the opportunity to be confronted by pastor Miller in these pages. Somewhere in this book he is going to get through to those who do!

But because of his out-front focus on the situation in the Reformed Churches, I am afraid that many others will neglect his work. That would be a mistake. I can think of few biblical studies of evangelism that would so inform, challenge and motivate any Bible-loving Christian more than this one. And— it might just be added—it is not only the Reformed Churches that have problems with evangelism!

Evangelism and Your Church, then, makes a solid contribution to the current evangelical scene. Above all, it is biblically well balanced: it is doctrinal and practical, negative and positive, convicting and encouraging. Read it!

Jay Adams
The Millhouse
Juliette, GA
1980

CHAPTER ONE

The Unspent Treasure: Our Missionary Legacy

Do you remember "Roots"? Few things captured the imagination of the American public so completely as that television chronicle of a black family's life. All of a sudden, people were scouring archives and attics for traces of their family history. Overnight, the past became the "latest thing." It was seen by thousands of Americans as the key to a deeper sense of personal identity.

I don't believe that the American public had ever experienced a phenomenon quite like "Roots," but it wasn't the first time I had seen large groups of people delve into the past with great curiosity and enthusiasm. As a pastor and seminary teacher during the past 20 years, I have seen that an interest in theological roots runs deep among Christians of almost every tradition. My own ministry lies within Reformed and Presbyterian circles. There I have observed many times that a recounting of our Reformation heritage will light up a Presbyterian countenance as little else would! Our historical roots are very important to us.

And really, isn't that as it should be? The events that spread the gospel through Western Europe should inspire doxologies in the person who loves God's Word. And the amount of praise lavished on our forefather John Calvin, in particular, justly honors the scholar, pastor, and teacher who embodied the Reformation commitment to a faith governed by the Word of God.

In my opinion, the Reformed community would be hard to surpass in the way it has respected and preserved its historical and spiritual heritage. And yet, one thing about our secular,

"Roots"-seeking counterparts challenged me regarding the manner in which we study our past. Above all other considerations, their interest in their pasts is supremely *practical*. They study their family histories because they believe that such knowledge will provide them with a perspective that will enable them to function better *today*. They are convinced that the past will open the door to the present, that it will help them to find perspective and purpose now.

Most of us would agree that these individuals are expecting too much from an assemblage of historical data. It is unrealistic to believe that one's past history will infuse meaning and purpose into a life which otherwise lacks them. As Reformed Christians, however, our position is different. Our individual and corporate lives *do* have meaning and purpose: to glorify God through the faithful ministry of the gospel of His Son, as it is contained in the Scriptures. We know why we are here; we do not need to look to the past to find that answer. However, I am convinced that a study of our religious heritage could be of immense instrumental value if we sought from it practical insights on the ministries of men like Calvin, Knox, Whitefield, and Edwards. What was their understanding of their ministries? How did their perspectives shape the form their works took? What of their perspectives and priorities may we adapt to our ministry in a twentieth-century setting?

I believe that we as Reformed believers need to ask questions like that today, because I think most of us would agree that the Reformed community has lost much of the impact it had on the world in other periods since the Reformation. It seems as if we are heirs to a vast spiritual inheritance, but we don't know what to do with it. We know it is valuable, so we guard it to keep it intact. But we lack the practical wisdom to take our fortune and reinvest it, so that the treasures of the past may yield new bounty in our generation as well.

A number of facts about present-day Reformed Christianity suggest that we have not fully "invested" our spiritual inheritance. Why, for example, are the vitality and fruit once seen in the work of men like John Calvin, John Knox, Jonathan Edwards, Gilbert Tennant, and George Whitefield so largely absent in Reformed circles today? Our greatest strength, theological scholarship, nevertheless lacks the impact it had on community and culture in Calvin's day. In foreign missions, we have fallen far behind other evangelical groups. Church growth here at home is taking place primarily among Baptist, independent, and Pentecostal brethren. More and more, the harvest Christ promised is being reaped by other reapers. Why should this be, when we as Reformed believers have certainly devoted ourselves to the "precious seed of the Word"?

Even more unsettling is what we see within some of our churches. Something has gone wrong when a friendly visitor attends one of our urban churches and comes out saying, as one did, "I agreed with the theology of the sermon, but the whole service carried the odor of death." Louie M. Barnes, Jr., a pastor in the Reformed Presbyterian Church, Evangelical Synod, sees a clear pattern of loss in most Reformed and Presbyterian churches. On the basis of available statistics, he reports that in 1974 "the average local church in the U.S." had "barely one nostril out of the water," with Reformed churches in most cases "experiencing the same nosedive in 'growth' rates."[1] Now is a time when we need to learn what it was that enabled men like Calvin, Whitefield, and Knox to see such blessing on their work.

As I have studied these men and their achievements in the ministry of the gospel, what has come through again and again is their conviction that the gospel, the Word of God, is *alive* and *active*, a message so powerful and so thoroughly irresistible when applied by the Holy Spirt, that it could not help but bear fruit in the salvation of souls. Their reverence for the Word and for the doctrines of grace was great, just as ours is today, but the difference between us is this: while our emphasis is on preserv-

---

1. Louie M. Barnes, Jr., *The Church and Her Ministry* (Pittsburgh: The Board of Education and Publication, Reformed Church of North America, 1976), p. 53.

ing true doctrine and defending the faith, theirs was on taking the gospel and going on the offensive, bringing God's message to men and conquering them in Christ. They wanted not only to preserve the gospel, but to put it to work, to see it change lives and expand God's kingdom.

Charles Haddon Spurgeon's ministry illustrates the perspective I am describing. The source of power for his preaching can be seen in this sermon excerpt:

> Oh, the power, the melting, conquering, transforming power of that dear cross of Christ! My brethren, we have but to abide by the preaching of it, we have but constantly to tell abroad the matchless story, and we may expect to see the most remarkable spiritual results. We need despair of no man now that Jesus has died for sinners. With such a hammer as the doctrine of the cross, the most flinty heart will be broken; and with such a fire as the sweet love of Christ, the most mighty iceberg will be melted. We need never despair for the heathenish or superstitious races of men, if we can but find occasion to bring the doctrine of Christ crucified into contact with their natures, it will yet change them, and Christ will be their king.[2]

It was said of George Whitefield (by no less a preacher than John Newton) that "he never preached in vain."[3] J. C. Ryle describes him as "the first to see that Christ's ministers must do the work of fishermen. They must not wait for souls to come to them, but must go after souls and 'compel them to come in.' "[4] What was his motivation? "Cry out who will against this my frowardness," wrote Whitefield, "I cannot see my dear country men and fellow Christians everywhere ready to perish through ignorance and unbelief and not endeavor to convince them of both."[5] And to what did Whitefield attribute the amazing fruit of his preaching? "I intend to exalt and contend for more and

2. Charles Haddon Spurgeon, *The Passion and Death of Christ* (Grand Rapids: William B. Eerdmans Publishing Co., 1970), p. 45.

3. J. C. Ryle, *Select Sermons of George Whitefield* (London: Banner of Truth Trust, 1958), p. 30.

4. Ibid., p. 31.

5. Arnold Dallimore, *George Whitefield Volume I* (London: Banner of Truth Trust, 1970), p. 338.

more," he once wrote of his future ministry, "not with carnal weapons—that be far from me—but with the sword of the Spirit, the Word of God! No sword like that!"[6]

Calvin also felt the divine imperative not merely to defend the gospel, but to preach it actively to men. In his commentary on John 4:34, he notes:

> The nature of Christ's office is well known—to advance the kingdom of God, to restore lost souls to God, to spread the Gospel and in short to bring salvation to the world. The importance of these things made Him forget meat and drink when He was tired and hungry. From this we receive no common comfort. It tells us that Christ was so anxious for men's salvation that the height of pleasure for Him was to attend to it; for we cannot doubt that He has the same attitude towards us today.[7]

What is common to these quotations, and to the men who wrote them, is the deep awareness of God's foremost intention for His Word and for the church to whom it is entrusted: It is intended to glorify His great name *in its orientation toward the salvation of the lost!*

God had a missionary purpose when He gave mankind His Word. His desire to reveal Himself to men pervades Scripture from Genesis to Revelation (Gen. 3:15; Rev. 22:17). The fervor of men like Calvin, Whitefield, Spurgeon, Knox, Edwards, and Newton to reach out to the world with the gospel came out of their embracing of that purpose as their own. This is what we need to learn from our forebears; indeed, this is what we need to learn from God Himself. We need to come to grips with God's missionary purpose for His Word. John Newton once commented that "Calvinism was one of the worst systems preached theoretically, but one of the best preached practically."[8] I fear

---

6. Ibid., p. 409.

7. John Calvin, *Calvin's Commentary, The Gospel According to St. John*, trans. T.H.L. Parker (Grand Rapids: William B. Eerdmans Publishing Co., 1959), vol. I, pp. 105-6.

8. *The Autobiography of William Jay*, ed. George Redford and John Angell James (London: Banner of Truth Trust, 1974), p. 569.

that Reformed Christians today have fallen into the error of preaching the doctrines of grace theoretically instead of preaching them practically and using the truths of Scripture to draw men to Christ. Instead of using the Bible as our instrument to draw men into fellowship with God, biblical doctrine has become our grounds to exclude those—even other believers—who disagree with us. Instead of using the Scripture as the sword of the Spirit to conquer men for Christ, we spend our energies defending it, as if it were fragile and easily broken. Yet we have seen throughout history that God's power and blessing have been most evident not on those who have assumed a defensive posture toward the lost of the world, but on those whose first concern is to see God save them.

I do not wish to dismiss the church's responsibility to guard her sheep from wolves teaching false doctrine. My problem lies solely with the assumption that such concerns must have first place in the normal ministry of the church. I am persuaded that this protectiveness overturns God's standard order for the church and its ministry. God's first priority for His church is to proclaim the gospel to the lost, bringing them to salvation. This is followed by a cultivation of the life and unity which that gospel produces among the people of the Lord Jesus. And finally, in that context, as a living testimony to the power of the Word, the church defends herself against error.

We know that Calvin shared our concern for true doctrine, but it is noteworthy that he did not suffer from the reversal of priorities from which we suffer. Calvin knew the Bible as a great missionary book in a way that few moderns know it. For him it was largely a book of promises centering on Christ's conquest of the nations through gospel preaching. This can be seen in his commentary on Isaiah 2:3, where he says that men out of "all nations" will be conquered by "the doctrines of the gospel" and stream to Christ. Commenting on the verse that follows, he adds:

> By these words he first declares that the godly will be filled with such a desire to spread the doctrines of religion, that

everyone not satisfied with his own calling and his personal knowledge will desire to draw others with him. And nothing could be more inconsistent with the nature of faith than that deadness which would lead a man to disregard his brethren and to keep the light of knowledge choked up within his own breast.[9]

Calvin was not slow to translate his own missionary vision into action. During the years 1555 to 1562, 88 men were trained and commissioned by Calvin as pastors to France. Additional works established in Holland and Scotland by men trained by Calvin were greatly blessed. In Scotland, the response to Christ was so overwhelming that one contemporary observed that "the sky rained men."

In other lands like Germany, England, Wales, Poland and Hungary, flourishing Presbyterian and Reformed churches were planted and strengthened by men trained in Geneva. Even such ardently Catholic lands as Italy and Spain were touched by their influence. An amazing zeal for Christ's cause and the glory of God were instilled in the men Calvin taught.

Yet somewhere in the years between Calvin's century and ours, our working theology has become abbreviated in a way that would have dismayed such a pioneer in missions. Our emphasis on the wonderful doctrines of grace has somehow come to mask and perhaps (in our own minds) even justify a deep-seated indifference to the lost. Evangelism, God's first priority for His Word and His church, has become a peripheral activity in the lives of many local congregations. Often it even raises eyebrows as a theologically questionable undertaking because it is so far afield of our usual defensive posture! Louie Barnes noted this attitude in his aforementioned report. Unlike other denominational leaders whose church rolls were shrinking, Barnes observed that Reformed churchmen "sense very little urgency in this situation." In fact, he says, "many of my colleagues believe that a rapidly expanding, active 'church' is

---

9. John Calvin, *Calvin's Commentaries, Commentary on Isaiah* (Grand Rapids: William B. Eerdmans Publishing Co., 1948), vol. I, p. 94.

proof positive that doctrinal or ethical compromise has certainly taken place.''[10]

I also have observed this attitude among my Reformed contacts. I recall an incident in which one man in a Reformed setting accused another of Arminianism. Asked to justify his charge, he replied simply, ''He does aggressive evangelism; that means he's Arminian.'' In another instance, a Reformed pastor was alarmed that Campus Crusade for Christ had come through his community and motivated many of his people to witness in shopping malls. His response was to teach a class in which he posited that church officers alone were intended to do evangelism.

Of course, these are extreme examples. But what concerns me is their roots in a widely held conviction that evangelistic zeal is suspect. The abuses and inadequacies of some evangelistic groups may fuel those feelings, but I firmly believe that the greatest reason for our antipathy to zeal is that we have overlooked, as Calvin did not, God's oft-affirmed intention to draw the lost to Himself through the proclamation of His Word.

If God's primary commitment to reveal Himself to the world is as clear as I have maintained, why have so many well trained godly and dedicated pastors missed it? I attribute this myopia to a ''remnant theology'' that makes the idea of aggressive evangelism seem pointless. One pastor defended the position this way: ''We must not be impatient with history. This is the day of small things; apostasy has reduced us to a remnant. We should really rejoice that ours is the privilege of purifying and strengthening these few.''

It is here that I must disagree. If I read my Bible correctly, a statement like that has no meaning for God's people since the event of Pentecost. Such a small vision simply does not square with the finality of Peter's bold announcement that the ''last days'' have come and that an age of fulness has dawned, with the Spirit being poured out abundantly ''upon all flesh'' (Acts 2:17). It closes the eyes of faith to the wonder of God's saving

---

10. Barnes, *The Church and Her Ministry*, p. 53.

purpose reaching out since Pentecost to embrace the nations. A remnant theology does not take into account the global promises of Isaiah, Ezekiel, Zechariah, John and Luke which began to be fulfilled at Pentecost.

If we as a Reformed community are to regain our strength, we need to recover a biblical theology of expectancy founded upon the knowledge that the sovereignty of God is not restricted to the salvation of a few individuals. Scripture clearly connects it to God's saving purpose as it relates to all the world, as evidenced in His own missionary character, as sealed in His promises, and as defined by His gift of all authority to the Son as the Lord of the Great Commission. Scripture's great message to man is the offer of life in Jesus Christ, and God's intention is that many hear the message and be saved. My purpose in this book is to outline the biblical basis for a "theology of missionary expectancy" and to suggest practical ways in which faith based on such a theology may revitalize our churches.

God's Missionary Character

From the beginning of biblical revelation, God makes it clear that He has a missionary concern for mankind. When Adam and Eve fled His presence after the fall, He called them to faith and repentance with the promise that their seed would be His people, and would someday produce a victor who would crush Satan's head (Gen. 3:15). We learn early too that God is a jealous God (Exod. 20:1-6; Deut. 4). In this commandment He declares that He alone is God, and in the second commandment that He cannot bear that the devotion which is His due be given to graven images. The God who reveals Himself in the second commandment is a missionary God who cannot rest until He has established a knowledge of Himself in every corner of the earth (Exod. 20:4-6; Deut. 4:23-24; Isa. 42:1-8; Num. 14:21; Isa. 11:9; 6:3; 40:5; Hab. 2:14). His message to the nations is, "I am the Lord, that is my name; my glory I will not give to another, nor my praise to graven images" (Isa. 42:8, NASB).

Sensitive to the nature of the second commandment, Jesus cleansed the temple at the beginning and close of His public ministry (John 2:13-22; Matt. 21:12-13). He understood that the new age had come and that the court of the Gentiles (where the vendors and moneychangers had assembled) must be purged so that the nations might draw near to God. The temple was being readied by its Lord to become a house of prayer for all peoples (Isa. 56:6-8; John 2:13-22).

This desire of God's to reveal Himself stems from His nature as an inexhaustible fountain of life. His immortality (or life) is not the endless, cold existence of Aristotle's Unmoved Mover, but a superabounding personal life, an immortality of boundless vitality, overflowing love and creative delight (I Tim. 1:17; 6:15-16). The astonishing fulness of physical life found in the earth, the air and the seas is eloquent testimony to God's nature (Gen. 1; Ps. 104). He is fulness of life and He delights in life (John 1:1-16). And though He hates all sin, He has no pleasure in the death of the wicked (Ezek. 33:11). The God who zealously seeks the glory of His own name also desires to impart His fulness of life to men (John 1:4; 5:26).

In John 4, we see more clearly how God's zeal for His own worship and His divine delight in imparting life come together. Here Jesus identifies the Father as the Great Missionary. He asks us to believe that He is seeking true worshipers among the wicked and alien of the earth (vv. 2-3, 16-18). He seeks their worship but He also imparts to them through the Son a spiritual life described as ''a spring of water welling up to everlasting life'' (v. 14, RSV). This living water is nothing less than the Holy Spirit shed forth at Pentecost by the exalted Lord Jesus (Acts 2:33; John 7:37-39).

God's Missionary Promises

Christ's advent is the ultimate expression of the Father's desire to reveal Himself to men (John 1:18). In his Son, the Father makes it clear to our faith that He is formally and totally committed to rescuing the nations from the bondage of sin and Satan, and turning vast multitudes into followers of the Lamb (Gen. 12:3; Gal. 3:8; Matt. 28:16-20). What is more, the Bible stimulates our faith in Christ's work by expressing it in the form of trustworthy promises: God promises to bring the fulness of Christ's life to mankind and to fill the world with His glory through the ministry of Christ's Spirit (Isa. 44:1-5; Joel 2:28-30; John 4:14; 7:37-39; 10:10; 15:1-11). In particular, these Christ-centered promises inspire us with the confidence that the harvest is plenteous (Luke 10:1-2), that the elect are a multitude that no man can number (Rev. 7:9), and that the cross reveals a saving mercy which confronts all men everywhere with God's desire for their salvation (John 3:16-17; I Tim: 1:15; 2:4-6).

The Lord of the Great Commission

These world-embracing promises have special significance for the church, for they all flow from the person and work of Christ as triumphant Lord of the Great Commission. As has often been noted, the Great Commission is Christ's missionary command directed to His body, but it is also an announcement of Christ's sovereign conquest of the whole earth and His expressed intention to claim every inch of it for the honor of the triune God. The Great Commission issues from Christ's conquest of all creation at the cross and the tomb, where He earned the right to all authority in heaven and earth (Matt. 28:18; Rom. 1:4; Acts 2:33-36), including the right to equip every believer with a Spirit of witness (John 15:26; 20:21-22).

The scope and fruitfulness of this work is anticipated by Jesus' first commissioning of His disciples at the Sea of Galilee. By their own efforts they had fished all night and taken nothing. But at Jesus' command, they took a mighty draught of fish, so that their "nets were breaking" (Luke 5:6, RSV). In this setting, Jesus announces: "Do not be afraid; henceforth you will be catching men" (Luke 5:10, RSV). This sign becomes a parable, then, of the kingdom harvest (Luke 10:1-2; John 4:35; 12:32).

By faith we expect rich harvest fields and breaking nets, for the gospel is specifically designed to bear fruit. It is the "word of truth, the gospel" which bears fruits among the Colossians, "as indeed in the whole world it is bearing fruit and growing" (Col. 1:6, RSV). In Acts we discover that the Word of the living Lord conquers sinners in Jerusalem and the priests in the temple (6:7), nullifies man's eloquence (12:20-24), subdues the Gentiles (13: 48-49), and reduces man's magic to ashes (19:17-20). His gospel conquers 3000 men at Pentecost, with 5000 more converted shortly thereafter, and makes the book of Acts to be what someone has called the New Testament book of Numbers because of its recording of the great numbers of conversions (6:7, 9:31, 42; 11:21, 24, 26; 12:24; 14:1, 21; 16:5; 19:20).

Our brief summary reveals that the God of the Scriptures has a passionate commitment to evangelism—His mighty, holy heart is in it all the way. Pentecost was God's graphic announcement that His saving intentions were now to be applied to the church and the world. The victory of the Lord over sin and death led to a "new birth" for the church as it was seized by God's own missionary purpose. In the words of Herman Bavinck, "On that day this church is born mission church and world church."[11]

Obviously, then, we are living out of touch with what God is doing in the age of the Spirit if we have no zeal for witness. We have become detached from roots much deeper than those that tie us to Calvin: we have cut ourselves off from the purpose of the Christian church since its inception. For this coldness we must repent and confess this sin particularly. Each pastor reading this chapter needs to own up to any sermons that were preached without concern for the lost and did not reflect any of God's saving purpose for men, to the failure to pray for unsaved hearers, to the forgetting of unsaved visitors coming to Lord's Day worship. Elders who do not labor full time in the Word also need to ask themselves about priorities. How often

11. Herman Bavinck, *Our Reasonable Faith*, trans. Henry Zylstra (Grand Rapids: William B. Eerdmans Publishing Co., 1956), p. 390.

their lives fall into patterns of such busyness or rigidity that they do not have time to witness! They find themselves reserving their zeal for their own affairs rather than God's purpose for the world.

Our hope for renewed vitality as a Reformed community rests on our willingness to expand our vision and align our faith with God's sovereign missionary purposes throughout the world. We need to ask Him to send His Spirit to instruct us on how to go with the gospel in a spirit of confident expectancy, rooted in His promises and the fulness of the working of the Holy Spirit. This believing expectancy is most crucial. Our participation in God's great world harvest initiated at Pentecost is founded in faith, and faith without expectancy is an empty shell, mere mental assent which means nothing before God. But faith filled with humble confidence in God's character and promises is the mark of the kingdom's presence and power. From this assurance comes a singleness of mind, a determination to get the gospel to men no matter what the cost.

CHAPTER TWO

How Big Is God's Mission Field?

A look at the universe about us reveals that God has a certain style: the massive and the majestic. God's workings in the spiritual realm follow the same pattern. It should not surprise us that the prophet Isaiah would refer to the coming of the Messiah as a "strange deed"—a work so earthshaking in magnitude that it would sweep away all evil and lay the foundation for a whole new order (Isa. 28:14-33; 52:13−53:12).

That is exactly what happened at the cross. It was not the place where, as Albert Schweitzer once concluded, Jesus was crushed by the wheel of history, but rather where the Son of Man took that wheel and reversed its whole direction.

At Calvary the demon powers lost their authority over the world (Col. 1:13; 2:15), the guilt of sin was cancelled (Col. 2:13-14), sonship was conferred upon all who believe (John 1:12), and the Holy Spirit was purchased for the life and sanctification of the church (John 1:29, 33; 7:37-39). God offers no tiny gospel. It is a work so great that no man can remain neutral before it. "And I," says Jesus, "if I be lifted up from the earth will draw all men unto me"(John 12:32).

The dimensions of God's deed of salvation should challenge us, convict us, and encourage us in our evangelism. Yet, as we saw in the previous chapter, many Christians, particularly those with Reformed convictions, act as if God's work at Calvary was very small. Their belief that God elects those who will be saved has led them too often to the unconscious assumption that the cross concerns only a few, and that the wisdom of offering it to the rest is questionable.

This is no minor snarl in our theology. In fact, I am persuaded that misconceptions here have led many Reformed pastors virtually to eliminate the gospel from their preaching. And though most of them would formally reject hyper-Calvinism as much as Arminianism, there is substantial evidence that they often preach and teach as if they believed it. At the very least they do not offer the cross to men with believable conviction or with pointed application to their hearts.

This criticism is not meant to minimize the importance of the doctrine of election. We are right to believe that Christ died with saving efficacy for His sheep alone. You cannot escape the particularity of great passages like John 10:15, where Jesus tenderly and emphatically announces His great love for His own people. The Lord means for us to understand that He really purchased salvation for His people and irresistibly applies it to their hearts. He did not buy them a hypothetical salvation or atone for the sins of all men.

But we make a great mistake if we think this is the whole story. It is an important part—indeed, it is the foundational part—but it should not be understood in a way that wipes out the reality of the free offer of the gospel and prevents the preacher or witnessing Christian from aiming the gospel directly at men. The particular design of the atonement must not be permitted to cancel out related biblical teaching that the cross is sincerely offered to all men everywhere.

God's saving purpose has a bearing upon all sinners in this world. "For God," says the Gospel of John, "did not send the Son into the world to condemn the world, but that the world might be saved through Him" (John 3:17). Paul says, "It is a reliable saying, deserving full acceptance, that Christ Jesus came into the world to save sinners, among whom I am the foremost" (I Tim. 1:15). He adds in the same Epistle that "God our Savior . . . desires all men to be saved and to come to the knowledge of the truth" (2:3-4, NASB).

From these passages we see that the primary goal of God's sending His Son to the world was not to condemn but to save.

His concern was clearly to bring salvation to a mankind under eternal condemnation. In the cross God faced us all with His astonishing deed of love. In the terse words of John Calvin, "The Heavenly Father does not wish the human race that He loves to perish."[1]

A study of John 3:16 helps to bring this truth to sharper focus. It seems obvious that this verse does not teach the Arminian view that Christ died with a saving efficacy for everyone, including Judas. It also should be clear that John 3:16 is not saying the same thing as John 10:15, where Jesus speaks about laying down His life for the sheep. What it says is that the gift of the Son by the Father represents His astounding love for all mankind. It is talking about the cross as God's supreme deed of loving confrontation with an evil world, and the cross as God's invitation to every man to receive this salvation by faith.

In a great sermon entitled "God's Immeasurable Love,"[2] B. B. Warfield argues that "the world" in John 3:16 does not refer to the whole of mankind as I have suggested, but to the evil *in* mankind. In effect, he believed that the elect are what is in view, as a "world" of depraved sinners, and hence the term "world" refers not to the whole race but to the sin of man in its intensity and depth.

The church is indebted to Warfield for spotlighting the awfulness of human depravity conveyed by the term "the world," but this does not prove that the "world" here can be limited to the elect. It takes a good deal of scholarly sophistication to draw such a conclusion from the text, and, even more important, the thematic emphasis of the passage does not fall on the design of the atonement for the elect, but on the greatness of the gift and its saving effect on all those who respond to the invitation in faith. What comes through to the reader is the Father's love in

1. John Calvin, *Calvin's Commentaries, The Gospel According to St. John*, trans. T. H. L. Parker (Grand Rapids: William B. Eerdmans Publishing Co., 1956, 1961), vol. I, p. 73.
2. B. B. Warfield, "God's Immeasurable Love," *Biblical and Theological Studies* (Philadelphia: Presbyterian and Reformed Publishing Co., 1952), pp. 505-22.

the matchless gift of His Son so that whoever appropriates this gift is granted eternal life as a present possession. John 3:16 does not close the door on anyone. It spells out the invitational character of John 3:14-15, which had climaxed with a statement of God's purpose to save *"whoever* believes in Him."

William Hendriksen takes up this point in his commentary on this great verse. He writes:

> God does not leave mankind to itself. He so loved the world that his Son, the only begotten, he gave, with this purpose: that those who receive him with abiding trust and confidence may have everlasting life. Though the gospel is proclaimed to men of every tribe and nation, not every one who hears it believes in the Son. But whoever believes— whether he be a Jew or a Gentile—has everlasting life. [3]

The universal character of God's offer in John 3:16 is also reinforced by the parallelism between "the world" and the race of men in the immediate context. In verse 19, for instance, we read, "And this is the condemnation, that the light has come into *the world,* and that *men* loved darkness rather than the light; for their deeds were evil." It appears inescapable that here "the world" and lost "men" or mankind are one and the same.

In short, what we discover in John 3:14-21 and the rest of the Gospel of John is that the covenant of grace has come to a world-embracing fulfillment. Centuries before, God had promised this to Abraham when He said, "In you all the families of the earth shall bless themselves" (Gen. 12:3; Gal. 3:8). In the gift of His Son the Father has wondrously fulfilled this global promise. The world with its terrible hostility to God is now invited to embrace this love. This invitational theme with its universal offer is announced at the beginning of this Gospel (1:7), forms the context for John 3:16 (3:14-15), and controls the use of major images in the book such as water, bread, and "lifting up" (i.e., the cross).

Yet too many Reformed scholars have ignored these promises

---

3. William Hendriksen, *New Testament Commentary, Exposition of the Gospel of John* (Grand Rapids: Baker Book House, 1961), pp. 27-28.

because their view of election does not really permit such a free and open gospel invitation. I believe that the text requires our affirmation of an indiscriminate offer of the gospel to men, but, whether you agree or not, you do need to see that a biblical doctrine like the definite atonement must not be permitted to silence the offer of the gospel or to leave it abstract and vague. The Christian who witnesses needs to know that God loves the world with a holy passion. We must be fully confident that God is really sincere in His love to wicked men, and that He desires our salvation with a most compassionate heart. With R. B. Kuiper, we must let John 3:16 grip us. In his words, "John 3:16 makes the amazing, incomprehensible unfathomably profound, well nigh unbelievable declaration that the Holy God sovereignly loves hell-deserving sinners, and that He loves them so much that He is willing that His only begotten Son, whom He loves with all the love of His infinite heart, should go to hell in their stead." [4]

If our witness does not reflect that burning conviction, our offer of the cross easily becomes a hollow charade. Our theology slips into a barren moralism and legalism. It weakens our own consciousness of our majestic God's infinite love and it leaves our hearers in unbelief and confusion. Our house of doctrine has walls, roof, and foundation, but it has no door by which faith may enter. The offer of the cross is the only way of access to God. Take that away and the sinner has no basis for hope, and every other doctrine will come across to him as burdensome law, hard and unsympathetic, with grace nothing but a bare word without content. But show him Christ, his door of access, and then he knows the way to go in and out and find rich pasture. As Calvin said, "We hold up this shield, that God does not want us to be overwhelmed in everlasting destruction, for He has ordained His Son to be the salvation of the world." [5]

5. Calvin, *Gospel According to St. John*, p. 75.
4. R. B. Kuiper, *God-Centered Evangelism: A Presentation of the Scriptural Theology of Evangelism* (Grand Rapids: Baker Book House, 1961), pp. 27-28.

Several years ago the implications of this for my preaching and witnessing became clear to me. Until that time I had never seen anyone converted through my pulpit ministry. I began to read the sermons of Charles Spurgeon, Walter Maier, and Martyn Lloyd-Jones. I also studied the messages in the book of Acts. Almost immediately I learned from the messages of men like Spurgeon that they knew how to summarize the gospel quickly and to point sinners directly to Christ. Along with this, I discovered that these men and the apostolic heralds in Acts preached to me in the second person. Sometimes they used "we" as one sinner speaking to another, but at the point of confrontation they took aim at particular men and said "you."

This startled me. My preaching had often been earnest, but it had been third person or first person exclusively—never a direct exhortation to come to Christ. But once I made the matter one of special prayer, almost immediately two people responded to the exhortation and showed evidence of new life. I had the same experience meeting people on a one-to-one basis. I began to ask, "Do you know personally about the love of God? Do you love Jesus because He died at Calvary for the sins of men?"

I had learned a great lesson: if you want to see men saved, it is your duty to aim the gospel directly at them. This is true of preaching from the pulpit; it is equally true of the use of an evangelistic booklet like "A New Life."[6]

Yet this leaves an important question unanswered. How does this offer of the cross relate to doctrines like unconditional election and particular atonement?

I suspect we often labor to force an artificial harmony between different lines of biblical teaching; nonetheless, God's truth *does* have a harmony. A missionary to Korea, Harvie Conn, resolved this apparent tension beautifully in his evangelism of prostitutes of his city. He began a Bible study on Ephesians 1, sharing with these women the truth of an electing

6. The purpose and use of the "New Life" booklet is explained in chapter 12 of this volume.

love that creates vessels of holiness for God. The stress fell on what God has done in Christ to beautify the undeserving, a message of special poignance to those involved in deep sexual sin.

It was not long before one of these wretched women would ask, "How can I have anything to do with this? You talk about holy lives that Christ is building, but that couldn't happen to me. I have fallen too far into sin."

The missionary made it clear that it is not what we do but what God has done in Christ to elect, purchase, and apply a salvation that matters. Then the question inevitably came: "How can I get this salvation?"

In response, the missionary took these despairing women to Ephesians 2:8-10 to show that faith is the way by which one enters into salvation. He would say something like this: "You are right to despair of ever being able to make yourself into a child of God. But if you put your trust in the Lord Jesus, you will be united to Him. You can then be sure that the Father elected you to holiness in Him before the foundation of the world, that Jesus died to save you eternally, and that the Spirit has forever sealed your salvation."

At the close of the final Bible study, Mr. Conn called on the women to follow him out the door of the brothel and run for their lives. "They were all held by chains of guilt," he said later, "but those who were persuaded that mercy and grace were meant for them ran."

This is the main point of this chapter. Sinners only run to Christ when they are persuaded that mercy is available to them. Our fears of "easy believism" and of "cheap grace" ought not to lead us to think that we should preach a hard discipleship which excludes sinners from mercy. This missionary rightly saw that each biblical doctrine should be presented in a way that preserves its evangelical character and shows sinners that grace is immediately available for every contrite heart.

Such an approach also unveils the underlying harmony between the preaching of Christ's death as a universal invitation and the truths of election and the definite atonement. The cross is offered indiscriminately to all who hear. God is sincere in this compassionate offer. At the same time, the universal call is made even more personal by teaching the hearer that Christ died with a special, irresistible design for His own sheep and that the hearer can know that he is one of them by trusting his life to Christ. The free offer of the gospel and the particular doctrines of sovereign grace are great friends. Do not make them enemies. Let them build your confidence in God's love for you, and then share with sinners the wonder of God's love manifested on a hill outside Jerusalem.

CHAPTER THREE

How Deep Is God's Love?

We have been examining truths that have given many Christians a zeal for witness that they never had before. I believe that God has few delights greater than to see His children go out with the gospel, confident of His commitment to evangelism and His promise of a harvest of barn-bursting proportions.

Yet we all know that it takes more than a formal knowledge of these things to motivate a believer to share his faith with the lost. Too many of us know "horror stories" about well-catechized churches which failed woefully in their witness to the unsaved. A pastor from a West Coast town remembers the night a man who had never been to church walked through the doors of a conservative Presbyterian church. The idea of visiting a church had so unnerved the man that he had taken several shots of whiskey to fortify his courage, and when he seated himself in the congregation, the unmistakable odor of drink wafted through the air around him. As his nearest neighbors sniffed in dismay, each one of them silently got up and moved.

"The man was left sitting in an empty circle. No one sat nearer than a dozen feet of him in any direction," the pastor recalled. "Understandably, he never returned. There was no chance to give him the gospel."

I don't know about you, but my first reaction to that story was to hope that such an attitude toward the world's "unwashed" was confined to that one unfortunate congregation. But, lest we reproach one church unfairly, we need to ask ourselves if things

22

would have gone much differently had the incident taken place in *our* churches. Can we say with confidence that we would have welcomed him? Had him home for supper? Put him up for the night? Given him money? Committed ourselves to extended counseling?

Only God can tell us truly how we have responded to the strangers He has sent into our midst. We may have done better than we think, or worse. But the Holy Spirit does convict us of sin for the times we have responded to a needy person with fear, or with a sense of alienation. God has called His church to be a welcoming church, to stand as His representatives on earth and welcome *everyone* to His heavenly banquet. He wants the love and compassion of the gospel to be heard from our lips. If we find ourselves unable to offer that welcome, to speak that message of love, to seek out those who need it, God wants us to realize something is wrong.

Well, yes, we concede, we can see that something is wrong. We need to pray for more zeal, more love, more boldness, more of a servant's heart, we say. But, no, God says, you are missing something even more basic. How do you respond instinctively to the drunkard, the adulterer, the drug addict? First, with fear for your physical safety, or for a schedule that may be irreparably disrupted if you become involved with such a person? And you also respond with a sense that this is someone with whom you have nothing in common, an alien creature who needs help in a way you never have. You think—perhaps unconsciously— that the gap that separates you in society places you in different categories with God as well. But that, says God, is where you are wrong. And this is the root of your problem with evangelism: you don't understand the gospel—for yourself or anyone else!

There are many professing Christians who have never fully grasped how lost in sin they really were, and how low God had to stoop to save them. The propriety and morality of their outward lives has made it hard for them to believe that their need

23

to be redeemed was as desperate as anyone else's. Certainly, they are convinced of their need for salvation, but the fact that their outward life has been unmarked by scandal or blasphemy has caused them to feel as if they don't need it quite as *much* as some other people they see.

This attitude toward the gospel, unarticulated though it may be, has two chief effects on the believer. The first is a distance between himself and God that, somehow, he is never able to overcome. He doesn't understand why; he believes the right things, he prays, he is active in church and is willing to serve. But the problem came about when he first placed himself partially out of the reach of the gospel and of grace. A person who has limited his need for God's grace has inevitably limited his relationship with God. God's unconditional, unlimited love for him is something he has never known. It is beyond the realm of his experience. He doesn't, at bottom, really understand what happened—for him—at the cross. And it is very likely that the gap he feels in his relationship with God is causing him either to try to earn God's favor with good works, or to rationalize away the richness of other people's Christian lives as maudlin, pietistic, or imbalanced.

It is easy to see that the second effect of such an attitude toward the gospel concerns the believer's relationship to the lost. A person who himself has not heard God's words of compassion to the lost cannot communicate it to others. If, in our own minds, we have limited our need for the gospel, we do not see ourselves as one with sinners in obvious need of saving grace. We feel removed from them, just as we feel removed from the full impact of the gospel. We don't understand that we, too, were the "unwashed" when God met us and saved us, and the distance we feel from both the gospel and those who need to hear it soon disengages us altogether from the enterprise of evangelism. Salvation? Well, it is God's covenant commitment to forgive, we say to ourselves, reducing the magnitude of God's work to match our experience of it. It will get done somehow. And the world? Well, it's pretty obvious that if those "unwashed" out there were really sincere about the gospel, they would clean up and get to work. Then we'd be willing to witness to them.

With many members in this frame of mind, what soon evolves is a church that exists for her own sake. God seems far away, and so do the lost, so the highest goal becomes the congregation's own comfort, order, and safety. Protected from the outside world by a double wall of elaborate doctrine and conventional worship, the church is never challenged about the spiritual void that threatens to consume her, because non-Christians can seldom make their way inside!

What a tragedy! And how hard it is to admit that it may be so with us! But our living Lord Jesus has powerful medicine to heal His church, if she is willing to acknowledge her need. That medicine is the gospel, as it really is, not as we have truncated it by our unbelief. We can be healed of our sins by learning afresh from the Holy Spirit about the riches of the message of Christ (Col. 2:9-10). Let us examine again some of the crucial points of the gospel message that we may have missed.

Paul defines the gospel as the "good news" or "good message" that "Christ died for our sins according to the Scriptures, and that he was buried; and that he hath been raised on the third day according to the Scriptures" (I Cor. 15:1-4, ARV). What confronts us in Paul's summary is a cross, i.e., a substitutionary atonement, and "our sins." They belong together. The cross represents God's assessment of the seriousness of our sin, and it is only when we see this that we can comprehend the fulness of grace displayed in the atonement, God's provision for the sins of His elect. A true perception of these two spiritual facts—the gravity of our sin and the infinite depth of God's grace revealed in the cross—is what we need most as Christians to make the gospel a transforming reality within us.

Those of us, especially, who have been spared a lurid past can gain a truer understanding of our profound need for the cross by considering our obligations to God as summarized in the first commandment: "Thou shalt have no other gods before me" (Exod. 20:3). The intent is not that God is to be put first, while all other things are to take second place. Rather, the commandment announces that God alone is God; there can be no second or third places for anyone or anything. Literally, the idea is that "You shall have no other gods in my sight" or "before my face."

This unyielding command requires complete surrender to God of all that I am and have. Do I own my house? My car? My family? Not really. I am only a steward of God's gifts. All that I have is to be immediately and completely at His disposal. Asaph caught the meaning when he cried, "Whom have I in heaven but thee? And there is none upon earth that I desire beside thee. My flesh and my heart faileth: but God is the strength of my heart and my portion forever" (Ps. 73:25-26).

Jesus rephrased it like this when asked what was the greatest or first commandment: "The first of all the commandments is 'Hear, O Israel, the Lord our God is one Lord: and thou shalt love the Lord thy God with all thy heart and with all thy soul and with all thy mind, and with all thy strength' "(Mark 12:29-30).

The first commandment is the foundation for all the others. It puts the "fear" or worship of God at the center of every "ought" in the divine law. It means that in keeping each of the other nine commandments, we must also return our heart's adoration to the living God. In keeping the sixth commandment, for example, I must not kill my neighbor in thought, word, or deed, but devote myself to furthering his welfare as though his life were my own. And, in doing this, I must act out of devotion to the God who has made us both.

The God-centered character of the law makes plain the extent to which man has fallen short of its holy requirements. When we face the law's exalted nature, we begin to understand, for example, that our present-day consumerism is more than "keeping up with the Joneses": it is rebellion against the Most High by taking His property and treating it as though it were our own by inherent right. As an habitual action it can only be described as a course of practical atheism. An overstatement? Not to God. I am by nature, therefore, the just object of God's wrath. I am part of that "world" addressed in John 3:16 just as much as any drunkard or adulterer.

Until we face our condemnation before the law and acknowledge our blindness and spiritual rebellion, too many of us Christians feel superior to the world's more conspicuous sinners, while blinded to the greatness of God's love to sinners at the cross. But if we take the first commandment in the manner God intended, we are *all* exposed as worldly to the core. We "clean-living" sinners are no less fallen than anyone else. It is the nature we have received from Adam that condemns us, and our own worldly habits reveal our kinship with our fallen father.

Yet the first commandment also illuminates the means of our healing: it makes clear why the Father so freely and righteously accepts the work of His Son on our behalf.

The answer lies in the quality of the Son's obedience. Eternally equal with the Father, the Son was commissioned by Him to take on our human nature and live and die in our place. This was an obedience of complete humiliation characterized by an exciting word—willingness. In the light of His own performance, the Son could say: "I delight to do your will, O my God. Your law is in my heart" (Ps. 40:8); "I have no other gods before you" (Matt. 4:10). It was His obedience to the first commandment that delighted the Father and required that He accept the Son's atonement as a matter of perfect justice (Phil. 2:1-11; Eph. 5:1-2). The Father in turn rejoiced that at last one man stood on the center of the stage of history who could say truthfully, "I love the Lord with all my heart and with all my soul and with all my strength and with all my mind."

Perhaps now we can sense something of the depth of God's love at the cross. In the person of His Son, the Highest came to save the lowest and lift us up to be with Him. His justice required that He dip the being of His only begotten Son into the

27

depths of hell for our sakes. As Thomas Kelly wrote,

> Many hands were raised to wound him,
> None would interpose to save;
> But the deepest stroke that pierced him
> Was the stroke that justice gave.[1]

We should expect that a confrontation between the God of the first commandment and us worldlings would unleash holy wrath upon us. But instead of a curse, we have been overwhelmed by the greatness of God's love.

Perhaps it seems strange for me to direct what is essentially evangelistic material to an audience concerned about mobilizing other believers to evangelize. But Scripture teaches that not everyone who claims to be part of God's people is really one of God's own (Matt. 7:21-27). Mere profession proves little if it is not accompanied by life change. Several years ago, a good friend of mine took a problem-ridden Presbyterian congregation as his first pastorate. For him to have exhorted the people to evangelism would have made little sense because he quickly saw signs that many of them were not converted themselves. He quietly embarked on a visitation program to evangelize each family, and before many months had passed, he saw over 60 couples turned to Christ.

There are other reasons, too, that I emphasize the gospel to those who say they already believe it. Too many of our church members may have been born again, but their knowledge of their sin and the grace of God is so shallow that, in a real way, they need the message of salvation to come into their hearts with something very like first-time conversion. And there is also a sense in which even more mature believers must confess that the world and the love of material comforts are too much with them. The first commandment continuously reveals that I have an unlimited need for a reconciling Savior. Though I have passed

---

1. Quoted from Thomas Kelly's hymn, "Stricken, Smitten, and Afflicted," *Selection 192, Trinity Hymnal* (Philadelphia: Orthodox Presbyterian Church, 1961).

from condemnation to pardon once-and-for-all, my sanctification *also* depends on my daily coming to Christ as a saved sinner (I John 1:8—2:6). God's gift of faith does more than effect my union with Christ by justification. It is also the Spirit's means to bring me back to Christ again and again for cleansing and filling at the fountain of life (Heb. 10:19-22; Rom 6; Ps. 51).[2]

Thus we see that God never intended to save us from our sins so that we would accomplish our sanctification in our own strength and witness out of this accomplishment. Instead, His Holy Spirit convicts believers of sin so that we will be drawn to the God of John 3:16 and the forgiveness available in His Son. A daily awareness that we must never stray from Calvary ourselves is the most important element in a God-honoring evangelism. As I experience the gospel as a message of God's total forgiveness, and Christ as the magnetic, personal center of my life, evangelizing with a gospel of forgiveness is a natural and inevitable outgrowth. It breaks down my pride; it reminds me of what God has done for me. And it is then that we find ourselves truly able to help someone like the whiskey-drinking visitor. What we offer to him is not social discipline which excludes him before he has an opportunity to hear about a reconciling Christ. Rather, having been humbled ourselves by our own present need, we approach the lost person with a new attitude. We have no desire to encourage him to continue in his sin, but to invite him to join us in going to Christ for total renewal. We want him to see with us the breadth and depth of the law of God as governed by the first commandment and then to experience the power of Jesus' blood to cleanse us and write God's law in our inmost being.

Approaching witness from this comprehensive point of view,

---

2. Cf. John Murray, *Redemption Accomplished and Applied* (Grand Rapids: William B. Eerdmans Publishing Co., 1955), p. 116. In this context, Murray is speaking primarily of repentance, but what he says of repentance also applies to faith in its on-going relationship to a living Christ. He says, "Christ's blood is the laver of initial cleansing but it also is the fountain to which the believer must continually repair."

we leaders can bring a fresh awareness of grace to our ministries. We will not be trying to train our people in something alien to them and to us. Personal witness and evangelism as an enterprise will issue from our delight in God and the appreciation of His grace in Jesus Christ. We will be able to receive strangers as friends, so that they may experience through us the welcoming attitude of Christ.

The infallibility of our message should lead to great confidence in our witness. Why then do so many Bible-believing Christians seem to lack it? They appear to believe all the right things about the Scriptures, yet I fear that, for many, the assent is simply mental; Christ is not a compelling reality in their lives. No wonder they hesitate to witness! We need to search our hearts for Pharisaism, for the sin of studying the Word as an end in itself for purely intellectual purposes (John 5:37-47). We want to escape Jesus' severe condemnation: "You do not have His word abiding in you" (John 5:38, RSV).

The antidote for such a powerless orthodoxy is to see by faith that Scripture is intended to lead us to God Himself through a living, reigning Jesus Christ. The Scriptures preach to us a living, risen Lord. And grounded in that firsthand knowledge of Christ, our testimony can convince men of the reality of our living Lord Jesus. I vividly recall an experience I had as a youthful unbeliever, steeped in intellectual despisal of the Christian faith. It was August 1945, and the atomic bomb had just been exploded over Hiroshima. As we commuters boarded our bus, people were shaking their heads and wondering whether this new weapon would destroy the world. A sailor responded quietly, "No, the world won't ever be destroyed by atomic bombs. Jesus won't let that happen. He's coming back first." As an unbeliever, I was completely silenced by this unquestioning confidence. It was biblical boldness, grounded on a certainty that came from the Spirit of God.

Confrontation, the third aspect of biblical boldness, flows from our certainty of Christ's sovereignty in the universe. Because we know for sure that the cross has given way to a crown, we are willing, indeed compelled, to confront men with the message of the gospel. We do this because we believe that the King's rights require submission to His living lordship.

Such a confrontation requires a clear statement of the message. A man cannot be confronted with Christ's redemptive rule until he sees its nature clearly and understands that it *requires* his conversion. Paul had this in mind when, in Ephesians 6:20, he asked for prayer that he might preach *"boldly,* as I ought to speak." In the parallel passage in Colossians 4:4, he makes the same request by asking "that I may make it *clear* in the way I ought to speak" (NASB). "Clear" and "bold" are virtually interchangeable terms here, and they remind us that confrontation is not a psychological domination or entrapment, but a presentation of truth that brings a person face to face with Christ.

Read the messages recorded by Luke in Acts. All of them are clear, specific, and confrontational in character. They touch men at their most vulnerable points. On the day of Pentecost, Peter bluntly rebukes his hearers as the murderers of the Son of God (Acts 2:22-23, 36). In Athens, Paul does not talk about the sins of the Jews but about the idolatry of the Greeks (Acts 17:22-24).

Such confrontation does not mean that we ignore good manners or that we force truth on men who are not ready to receive it. We must be quick to respect human dignity and deal with questions in patient humility. But we also take it as a God-given norm that the work of evangelism requires us, as one evangelist has said, to stand "directly before the heart's door of a sinner and clearly" confront "him with the gospel of Christ."[2]

One older teenager in our congregation does this by picking up hitchhikers and greeting them in the following friendly way: "Hello, I'm Richard Doe, and I want to share with you that Christ is alive." The quality of the ensuing conversations is usually excellent, and hitchhikers confronted in this way rarely give trouble.

Another member, a truck driver, visits hospitals. He often opens a conversation like this: "My reason for visiting you is to let you know about the love of Jesus, that there is nothing better in the whole world than knowing Him." In one instance, five members of a family were brought to Christ through reading a

---

2. C. E. Autrey, *Basic Evangelism* (Grand Rapids: Zondervan Publishing House, 1959), p. 27.

Bible he left with a dying young man.

We are also blessed with two young women who visit nearby college campuses. Their approach has been simply to introduce themselves to students and ask, "May we have a few minutes of your time to talk to you about Jesus Christ and the new life He gives?" A number of students have been converted through their ministry.

What we seek, in short, is to get enough truth before men in a personal, loving manner that they may see their responsibility to act before the hour of opportunity has passed. A witness empowered by biblical boldness is clear, compassionate, confrontational, and confident: confident that the Holy Spirit who inspired the testimony will also apply it to the hearts of those who hear.

CHAPTER FIVE

Prayer and the Promises: Power Source for Bold Ministry

The book of Acts makes it plain that the bold witness described in the previous chapter is God's normal for His church. After Pentecost, we see that Peter and John are characterized by incredible courage in proclaiming the good news (Acts 4:13), and they do not stand alone. Stephen's fearlessness in witness and debate surpasses even the boldness of the apostles (Acts 6−7). The same fervent tongue is also found in the church as a whole. Believers are not silenced by persecution. Instead, those "who were scattered went about preaching the Word" (Acts 8:4, RSV).

How did this happen? In the Old Testament, God's bold ones were few in number. How, suddenly, did the whole church of God begin to function like God's special prophets of old? The answer lies in the coming of the Holy Spirit, the Spirit of witness who, as He indwells men and women, enlists and equips them to do His work.

There is something else too: the means God provides to appropriate the Spirit's power in our lives. That means is prayer. It is our door of access to the Heavenly Father through which, as His adopted sons and daughters, we receive His grace to do His work. And, again, it is the Holy Spirit who brings our prayers to the Father.

The coming of the Holy Spirit and the believer's consequent new access and power in prayer are what make the difference between the Old Testament church and New Testament church. Under the old covenant, God's people were notorious for not stirring themselves up to pray (Isa. 64:7). But Christ's resurrection and ascension ushered in a new age when His people were indwelt by the Spirit of prayer, who warms our hearts to approach the Father and who makes intercession for us so that our prayers may be heard. The church pictured by Luke is first and foremost a confident, expectant church because it is a praying church. These Christians had been shown the vital link between prayer and the work God gave them to do. They knew:

— that the Lord taught His disciples to seek the gift of the Spirit through earnest prayer (Luke 11:1-13);

— that the Lord commanded His disciples to wait in Jerusalem until they were filled with the power of the Spirit (Luke 24:49);

— that His disciples obeyed the Lord by waiting in constant and united prayer for the coming of the Holy Spirit (Acts 1:13-14; 2:1-4);

— that the disciples were filled with the Spirit while they prayed at Pentecost (Acts 2:1-4), and subsequently when they sought power to confront a hostile world with renewed boldness (Acts 4:22-31);

— that the apostles were unalterably committed to prayer as their first priority in ministry (Acts 6:4);

— and that one of the four distinguishing features of their newly born church was its being devoted continually to the practice of public prayer (Acts 2:42). [1]

In short, what the church of Jerusalem had discovered was that the work of the gospel required the gift of the Spirit's filling, sought in fervent prayer. Without this heavenly anointing, there is only an earthly work. Our words have no power unless the Spirit speaks through us, and they have no effect unless the Spirit applies them to men's hearts.

It is sad today that many believers who are sensitive to

1. Cf. Harvie M. Conn, "Luke's Theology of Prayer," *Christianity Today* XVII, (December 22, 1972), 6-8. I also wish to acknowledge Professor Conn's lectures on prayer given at Westminster Theological Seminary as contributing to these insights.

doctrinal issues are often insensitive to the vital link between evangelism and prayer. They emphasize the power of the written Word, but have less awareness of the necessity for united and continued prayer that God would apply the Word to sinners through the Spirit. Commonly, these orthodox Christians have a certain fear of fervent public prayer among believers. Not only are they afraid of displays of ''enthusiasm,'' but they feel that the main task of the church at this end time is to hold the line, to maintain true doctrine, and to wait for God—rather than petition Him—to accomplish His sovereign good pleasure in the area of evangelism.

These believers are perfectly right in their determination to maintain the faith in our time. Perhaps that is why it is difficult for them to see that they are actually heretical when it comes to the doctrine of prayer. But it is a most serious deviation in doctrine to neglect the teaching that all Christian work hinges on the supplication of God's people and ''the supply of the Spirit of Jesus Christ'' (Phil. 1:19).

Then there are other believers who are sensitive to the importance of prayer, but who tend to think of it almost as a commodity, a vehicle for carrying forward the next evangelistic campaign. These zealous Christians are so intensely concerned with enlisting ''prayer support'' for the work that they stand in danger of equating prayer support with other kinds of support—material means and organizational structures.

Again, these believers are perfectly right in their recognition of the necessity of prayer. But this proper emphasis may well mislead them into thinking that they need no further instruction on the wonder of our access to the living God through Christ. As a result, they are robbed of the blessing of further growth in the doctrine of prayer. They may unwittingly fall into the grave error of attempting to manipulate God as did Israel in the days of Eli (I Sam. 4).

Christians in both situations have missed the exciting link between prayer and God's purposes in the world. It is, simply, that *prayer starts the promises of God on their way to*

40

fulfillment! In prayer, God allows us to lay hold of His purposes as these are expressed in His promises. Each promise is a hook for pulling our faith into the heavens. There we catch God's missionary vision of a world filled with His praise (Ps. 67). By claiming God's promises as we petition Him in prayer, we set God's work in motion (Luke 10:1-3, Acts 4:23-31). Unbelievable as it may seem, the omnipotent God permits our requests to activate the fulfillment of His mighty promises in history (Rev. 8:1-5). As the laborers pray, He begins to ripen the harvest for reaping (Acts 13:1-4).

As a leader in the colonial church, Jonathan Edwards understood this principle better than most. In the late 1740s he reasoned in an essay entitled "An Humble Attempt to Promote Explicit Agreement in Prayer" that revival and missionary outthrust inevitably resulted from believers committing themselves unitedly and continuously to intercession for this purpose.[2] As an example, he cited the experience of the revival through prayer of the Cambuslang Presbytery in Scotland. In his view, this and other mighty outpourings of the the Spirit did not happen by caprice, but came about because of the inherent connection between prayer and the descent of the Spirit. In essence, he taught that a concert of prayer to claim the biblical promises resulted in the fulfillment of great passages like Zechariah 8:20-23. There verses 21 and 22 picture a great concert of prayer by God's people and verse 23 reveals the result, when many men from the nations take "hold of the skirt of the Jew" and commit themselves to the living God.

According to historians of revival, Edwards' teaching on this subject stimulated a whole series of revivals and conversions throughout the 1700s. By the close of the century, American Christians came to understand that coldness and timidity in evangelism in the church could only be cured by a commitment

---

2. Jonathan Edwards, "An Humble Attempt to Promote Explicit Agreement and Visible Union of God's People, in Extraordinary Prayer, for the Revival of Religion and the Advancement of Christ's Kingdom on Earth," *Works* (Worcester: Isaiah Thomas, Jr., 1808), vol. III, pp. 355-494.

to corporate prayer. According to J. Edwin Orr, a major student of revivals, this ''concert of prayer'' became the dynamic source of boldness in evangelism and missionary endeavor for the U.S. right up to the mighty spiritual explosion of 1858. He says,

> The concert of prayer remained the significant factor in the recurring revivals of religion and the extraordinary outthrust of missions for a full fifty years, so commonplace was it taken for granted by the Churches. [3]

Bold praying has its impact on the individual as well. We have seen that such intercession brings the harvest to fruition by claiming the promises of God; it also becomes the power that activates the laborers. The reason for this is that boldness in witness is fed by boldness in worship and intercession. Left to ourselves, we Christians are not in the habit of witnessing. Our habitual relationships with friends, relatives and co-workers are ones of conventional reserve. But, when we have spoken first with God and claimed the promise of the Spirit's power and presence, we cannot be silent before men.

Prayer with this kind of boldness and power depends upon our understanding of Christ's work for us. We can pray this way only when we understand that the blood of Jesus has given us free access to the Father. Listen to Hebrews:

> Since therefore, brethren, we have confidence [boldness] to enter the holy place by the blood of Jesus, by a new and living way which he inaugurated for us through the veil, that is, His flesh, and since we have a great high priest over the house of God, let us draw near with a sincere heart in full assurance of faith, having our hearts sprinkled clean from an evil conscience and our bodies washed with pure water (10:19-22, NASB).

Jesus' work introduced a new day in God's relationship with man. The veil of the Old Covenant between a holy God and unholy men has been forever removed by the sacrifice of God's

---

3. J. Edwin Orr, *The Fervent Prayer: The Worldwide Impact of the Great Awakening of 1858* (Chicago: Moody Press, 1974), p. xi.

Christ. Now there is nothing between. Friendship, openness, access and freedom describe the new relationship between the Father and those who know Him through His Son. Hence boldness in worship is nothing but the sons of God exercising their new rights through the power of the Spirit.

These new rights, however, cannot be exercised in the absence of a clear conscience. We are exhorted to draw near "having our hearts sprinkled clean from an evil conscience" (Heb. 10:22, NASB). The tense of the verb in the Greek implies a past action extending into the present in its effect. This is what Jesus' blood has done for us. His past action has accomplished our permanent acceptance as sons with the Father. It also provides for a continued cleansing of the conscience through the daily confession of sins on the basis of that finished work. This is how we learn to enjoy the full freedom Christ has purchased for us, and it is the only way a Spirit-empowered evangelism can proceed unhindered by barriers of selfishness, unrepented sin and a guilty conscience. When the Spirit worked powerfully in Isaiah's life to make him a man of courage, it began with the man's immediate confession of a particular sin—a sin of the lips. He had become honest about himself for the first time, and in a most public way. It is this kind of repentance that prepares the way for bold prayers of faith, and a bold witness fulfilling those prayers.

CHAPTER SIX

The Community of Joy:
The Special Power of a Corporate Witness

One of the most astonishing aspects of the birth of the church in Jerusalem goes virtually unremarked by its historian, Luke. Consider the vitality of this newly born congregation: it attracts more permanent disciples in several weeks than did Jesus in three concentrated years of ministry in Judea and Galilee! How amazing that feeble men should see more fruit than the Lord Himself while He was on earth! Yet it is clear that this was God's intention. Holy "fear came upon every soul" who came upon the church in those days (Acts 2:43). By God's hand, men were daily compelled to faith by the supernatural quality of the church community (Acts 2:47).

What we see here is the fulfillment of Jesus' promise that those who believed in Him should accomplish greater works than He did during the days of His earthly ministry (John 14:12). And it is clear from Luke's account that the Holy Spirit used the *community* of believers, Christ's body, to perform that multiplication of Christ's work. Their witness together was powerful in the hands of the Holy Spirit.

We have seen in the past few chapters the way in which the Holy Spirit applies the gospel message to make individual believers bold in worship and witness. What Luke has recorded in Acts shows us that He does the same thing for Christ's people *as a body*. As the Spirit leads us into a deeper understanding of Christ's work on our behalf, our life as a witnessing community becomes a formidable testimony to the power of God.

44

Paul supplies a striking illustration of the way this happens in his first letter to the Corinthians. Concerning a church service even in that backslidden congregation, Paul could write: "But if all prophesy, and an unbeliever or an ungifted man enters, he is convicted by all, he is called to account by all; the secrets of his heart are disclosed; and so he will fall on his face and worship God, declaring that God is certainly among you" (I Cor. 14:24-25, NASB). Paul simply assumes that any normal worship service will lay bare the hearts of the unconverted and cause them to repent before the living God.

How could Paul have such confidence? The answer can only be that he understood the Holy Spirit's purpose in planting the church in the world. The church in its richness of gifts and graces is Christ's sole missionary representative among men. In its corporate life and rich diversity of gifts working by love, it is the image of Christ to the world, God's ambassador by which He makes Himself known to man. That is why in another astonishing passage, the apostle actually calls the church of God "Christ." In I Corinthians 12:12, he says, "For as the body is one and hath many members, and all the members of that one body, being many, are one body: so also is Christ." Logically, what you would expect as the climax of Paul's analogy between the unity and diversity of the human body and the nature of the church would be: "So also is the church." Instead, Paul gives the church the most sacred name of all. To be sure, he is not teaching that the church is Christ's actual continuing incarnation. But he daringly emphasizes that the fulness of gifts in the body derives all its reality from Christ, and that it is His personality shining through the body of believers into the world. Thus it is fitting that the church be named after the source of its holy light.

If we accept the Christological nature of our corporate life, those of us who lead must modify the way we train believers to think of witnessing. I am thinking of the image of evangelism as fishing for the lost. Too often we have only stressed the single fisherman with his pole. There is certainly a place for him, but

45

there is a danger that the "lone angler" concept will place undue emphasis on witnessing skills, techniques and special gifts, discouraging Christians who lack these distinctive features. It is clear that for the church in Acts, evangelism was something that involved everyone—and they were often involved together. We need to focus on the biblical metaphor of fishermen pulling together on the same net. Our shared life as the company of Christ's redeemed is at the very center of our gathering in of the lost.

This principle came to life for me in a rural pastorate I served some years ago. The church had had a history of conflicts widely known in the community and had a very poor reputation. But many in the church were sick of the strife and responded to the Spirit under the preaching of the gospel. As a body they began to look and act more like Christ. Gossip died down. The gifts of the Spirit began to flourish. The deacons faithfully sent flowers to any hospitalized sick in the community. Hot meals were taken to chronically ill persons. A spirit of prayer and intercession began to come on the prayer meetings. Visitors were impressed by a new attentiveness in the Sunday worship services. One of them remarked, "Before when I visited, everybody read their bulletins or just looked around. But now they listen like hungry people. The change is so mysterious, it's frightening."

Good things replaced bad when people talked about the church, and as a consequence, within a few months the size of the congregation had nearly doubled. I realized that the Lord had permitted me to see a major principle of Christian leadership: to get out of the way and direct all the attention to what Christ has done for us in the gospel and to what He is now doing to beautify us in His own image. In this context, witnessing is fundamentally "gossiping" about the glory of the cross and its imprint on the life of Christ's people.

The church today faces two main problems when it comes to our corporate witness. The first is the hampering of our missionary oneness by our highly individualistic lives. Our thinking is so often self-centered that our oneness and mutual love in the Spirit is suppressed. We lose the vital unity and deep caring which belong to us because of our union with Christ. A congregation living according to what God says is normal, and reflecting Christ's love by the Spirit's power, would unfortunately strike most of us as exceptional—and maybe a little bit strange!

The second problem is an extreme in the other direction. It is the kind of corporate identity which conceals the power of Christ. It is a corporateness which is closed, exclusionary and mechanically ritualistic. If you belong to the group, you are an "insider"; if you do not, you're an "outsider." There may be a measure of outward warmth in welcoming strangers, but basically the congregation is a closed tribe which demands a social change as well as a conversion of anyone who wishes to join. One can hardly be accepted as full member of this kind of body without learning a specialized religious vocabulary, embracing a narrow sectarian mindset, and often adopting a particular style of dress.

Happily, the Christian pastor need not despair if he sees his congregation victimized by these errors. The Scripture is on your side, and God's sword is readily available to cut away both of these destructive tendencies. The Apostle Peter deals forcefully with both errors when he sets forth the biblical basis for a community witness and identity. He writes: "You are an elect race, a royal priesthood, an holy nation, a people for God's own possession, *in order that* you may shine forth the excellencies of him who called you out of darkness into his marvelous light" (I Pet. 2:9). Here the apostle exposes a selfish individualism. Four times he gives us names which call attention to our being one people and not self-serving loners. We are in our origin, a race chosen of God, not just elect individuals; in our dignity, priests together near to God, not just single worshipers; in our sanctity, one nation separated by God from the world, not just single citizens of the kingdom; and in our being, common property owned by God, not just single members of his body. Furthermore, the subordinate conjunction translated "in order

47

that" makes very clear that we do not exist for ourselves as a local congregation or a particular denomination.[1] Our purpose, our reason for being, is to "shine forth the excellencies of him who called us out of darkness into his marvelous light." We have been redeemed from the self-exalting and self-serving spirit of tribalism. Our very existence in the world involves our shining into the world's darkness. Tribalism makes everything center on preserving the status quo. It even perverts care for one another into a clannish self-love. But Peter confronts our self-ishness with God's great "in order that." As God's "new people," we are present among men *in order that* we together may represent Christ to them through our united praise of God.

I believe that there are four key ways in which our corporate witness can demonstrate the transforming power of Christ.

I. *Our United Testimony:* Our verbal testimony to the truth of the gospel is grounded in our conscious identification of ourselves as the people of God. We are called to affirm that we are united in our identity as the people Christ redeemed from the spiritually nameless of the earth. Together we await our glorious inheritance in our coming King (I Pet. 1:3-9).

This united witness to Christ's present lordship and imminent return has more than pyschological value for the believer. It also carries special weight in establishing the truth of the gospel before a doubting mankind. Scripture states that truth is established by the testimony of those who know and have seen. Such a testimony requires corporate validation; a single reporter is not enough. It was for that reason that the Lord chose a college of 12 to testify to the reality of His bodily resurrection. Later, He called the whole church to give united testimony to the transforming power of His resurrection. The churches that grow most rapidly today are the ones that understand their mission. As they are gripped by a joyous certainty about Christ's reality, they offer convincing testimony to unbelievers around them. The

1. Cf. Johannes Blauw, *The Missionary Nature of the Church; A Survey of the Biblical Theology of Mission* (South Pasadena, California: William Carey Library, n.d.), p. 132.

48

subsequent conversions have much to do with the church's stand *together*.[2]

II. *Our Worship:* Our corporate worship is another way in which Christ's reality and power are demonstrated to the world. Wherever the gospel is preached in the power of the Spirit, life-transforming effects inevitably follow (I Thess. 1:5-10). As believers in assembly hear the gospel of Christ, they are led to adore Him. By faith they confess their sins to God and to one another (Prov. 28:13; I John 1:8-10; James 5:16). To prevent hardness of heart they submit to mutual exhortation (Heb. 3:6-13). In addition to responding to the Word proclaimed by ordained officers, they use the Scriptures to teach one another with the wisdom distributed throughout the body by the Holy Spirit (Col. 3:16). In this body-life setting, God is so evidently at work that, as we noted before, the casual visitor is brought to conviction of sin and conversion as "the secrets of his heart are disclosed" (I Cor. 1:24-25, NASB).

Furthermore, this gathering of God's people is no ordinary fellowship. Here God meets with His people in heavenly fellowship, angel hosts converge, and Satan and his allies flee as lives are renewed. The holy is here and it is all-conquering.

In such a setting we hardly need to command witnessing. We only need to channel the zeal stirred up by the Spirit. Having said this, however, we must acknowledge that we cannot assume that every gathering of God's people will experience the fulness of His presence. Even a quick reading of Revelation 1−3 will show that it is all too easy to suppose that God is with us when He is not. Hence as leaders we must raise up constant prayer for every last one of our meetings, that they will be real meetings with God, resulting in changed lives. The whole point of the history of redemption is that when Immanuel is present, transforming deeds follow. Things human are turned upside down. When God is truly present in a worship service, we can

---

2. Note Acts 2:32 and I John 1:1-5.

be sure that the Word of God will be sanctifying believers and converting non-Christians.

III. *Our Ministries of Mercy:* The church's understanding of herself as "once . . . no people" who are "now the people of God" determines not only our actions *before* the world, but *with* unbelievers around us as well. Perhaps the most important way is our diaconal care of the poor. Through it, we act out by deeds of love the message of the gospel. For what is that message? It is that the Highest became the lowest to lift us up from the depths of sin into the riches of His royal palace. As recipients of this abundant mercy, we are compelled by our newfound wealth in Christ to share it verbally and practically in deeds of kindness to the widow, the orphan, the sick, and the poor. This is the emphasis of James 1 and 2, the theme of Romans 15 and II Corinthians 8 and 9. It is also the story of church history. Be it the Reformation or the Great Awakening, history shows that revival expresses itself in a concern for the weak which brings many of them to Jesus Christ.

IV. *Our Hospitality:* Closely allied to our care of the poor is the use of hospitality to express our community witness to men. We are right to seek to care for the needy and bring them to Christ. But the needy don't want our material gifts dropped in their laps, so to speak, from a speeding car! Our material gifts and our gift of the gospel are accepted as we also offer ourselves to them in hospitality. Biblical hospitality has escaped the pretensions of social entertaining which seeks to present the hosts to their best advantage; rather, it provides the occasion in which the hosts may share themselves as they are, in the simplicity of their dependence on Christ and in the profusion of love and gifts they have received from Him.[3]

There is no question that such hospitality is often trying for middle-class Christians. It is why many Christian homes have

3. Two helpful popular guides for biblical hospitality are Karen Burton Mains' *Open Heart, Open Home* (Elgin, Illinois: David C. Cook Publishing Co., 1976) and Edith Schaeffer's *L'Abri* (Wheaton: Tyndale House Publishers, 1969).

never hosted unsaved guests; it is why many evangelical churches have fled "changing neighborhoods" for the suburbs. The dispossessed of the earth are often the unwashed, and sometimes they are the destructive. Nevertheless, Scripture makes it clear that we can't worry about our image in the neighborhood or the wear and tear on our furniture. We must go ahead and invite them, and trust the Holy Spirit to help us to love them.

The same principle applies to our response to visitors to our services. People of all kinds come when they have been truly welcomed. But his welcome cannot have reservations. A smile in the sanctuary is not enough; we must be willing to welcome them into our homes too. In this domestic setting the common faith of God's people takes visible and natural expression. No matter what sort of evangelism your church undertakes—door to door, open air, or special revival meetings—you will lose the people your efforts bring in if they are not fully welcomed with the dignity and love God intended the church to offer them.

The four areas set forth in this chapter as basic to our corporate witness may seem elementary, even insignificant. Certainly they lack the drama of open air evangelism and similar outreach efforts. But what is basic to all our evangelism is that God calls every believer to witness in and through the body of Christ in natural ways. The challenge facing the church—particularly its leaders—is to avoid the trap of concentrating on personal evangelism and forgetting about the witness that the Holy Spirit has ordained for the church as a body. It is a big challenge, and satanic opposition is great. Many pastors have yet to preach the gospel plainly in their worship services. The formalism of church tradition has entombed many church meetings. Church buildings have become "consecrated" property that cannot be used for community outreach. Entire denominations have replaced the primacy of gospel preaching with an emphasis on upholding doctrine. Yet in all this, the gospel and the Spirit will be triumphant. God's purposes are such that the church will realize her purpose in the world, though some branches may be broken off in the blindness of their self-righteousness. The great fact that the church is Christ in the world cannot be displaced. The excellencies and deeds of God will shine into the world's darkness through our combined proclamation.

CHAPTER SEVEN

The Pastor as Model for Personal Witness

The picture of evangelism we have sketched here—the transformed believer boldly sharing his faith, the church united in a powerful demonstration of the gospel at work—may be as much the source of dismay as encouragement to a pastor with an unresponsive church. The fear, the apathy, the unbelief may be so great among the people you serve as pastor that the vision seems unattainable. You are hesitant to initiate even the most preliminary evangelistic efforts for fear that if they fail, any faint flicker of interest in witness would go out altogether.

But things need not go this way. Your efforts at evangelism can yield permanent habits of witness if you proceed along biblical lines. What are these biblical principles? The most important one is perhaps the simplest: learning by example. The central example for witness in the Scriptures is the church officer. The people are expected to imitate him (Phil. 3:17; I Thess. 1:6).

Note the pattern in the history of the New Testament church as set forth in Luke and Acts. First, the Great Commission is given to the Lord's disciples: ''Repentance and forgiveness should be preached in his name to all nations, beginning at Jerusalem'' (Luke 24:47, RSV).

Now consider how the apostles set the pattern after Pentecost. We saw in chapter 5 that they became models for witness by boldly preaching the gospel in Jerusalem (Acts 2−5). Stephen followed their pattern, preaching with even greater boldness than they (Acts 6−7). Apparently he perceived the new universal character of the church even before the apostles had seen it. As members of the Jerusalem congregation saw the example of apostolic boldness intensified in Stephen, they imitated their leaders when the church came under persecution (Acts 8:1,4).

I do not believe that Luke's recording of these developments is casual. It is an integral part of the plan of the book of Acts which, in large part, is governed by Jesus' outline of the Great Commission in Acts 1:8: "and you shall be my witnesses in Jerusalem and in all Judea and in Samaria and to the end of the earth" (RSV). The scattering of the congregation into Judea and Samaria is the initiation of the second stage of the Lord's fulfillment of His own missionary mandate. And in carrying this work forward, the Spirit now uses not the apostles, but the people generally (along with evangelists like Philip).

What the Spirit wants us to see is that the work of the Great Commission begins with the leaders, but it is also His good pleasure to have the whole congregation fulfill this ministry through the sovereignty of the Spirit. And in this early period of church history, let us note that the people appear far more willing than the apostles to fulfill the terms of the Great Commission (Acts 8:1-4). They are the ones to seek out the Gentiles without having the Gentiles initiate the encounter (Acts 11:19-24). In the setting of the contemporary local chuch, the parallel would be for the pastor and elders to begin evangelizing the middle class community only to have the rest of the congregation spontaneously reach out to black and Jewish neighbors as they caught the vision.

The same situation prevails later in Thessalonica. Into this European setting Paul and his missionary associates come and preach the gospel with great power and authority (I Thess. 1:5).[1] Then the people "having received the word in much tribulation, with the joy of the Holy Spirit," become imitators of the

---

1. For what follows, see Carl Kromminga, *Bringing God's News to Neighbors* (Nutley, New Jersey: Prebyterian and Reformed Publishing Co., 1976) and William Hendriksen's *New Testament Commentary, Exposition of I and II Thessalonians* (Grand Rapids: Baker Book House, 1955), pp. 48-57.

missionaries and the Lord (I Thess. 1:6, NASB).

This imitation included an amazing boldness in witness. "For," writes Paul, "the word of the Lord has sounded forth from you, not only in Macedonia and Achaia, but in every place your faith toward God has gone forth, so that we have no need to say anything" (I Thess. 1:8, NASB).

What a remarkable situation! Paul has brought the gospel to the Thessalonians and they function as an amplifier which rebroadcasts the gospel throughout the region of the eastern Mediterranean. Thus when Paul arrives in a new place, it seems that these Thessalonians had been there before him.

This recurrent pattern illustrating God's principles of evangelism also explains much about the contemporary evangelistic scene.

The first point: Ultimately, it is the Holy Spirit who fulfills the missionary mandate, but He has established a pattern for us to follow. The people evangelize when they have *been* evangelized. They also evangelize when they see their leaders evangelizing.

As pastor you really have no reason to hope that your people will become zealous for evangelism any other way, for the example of church officers plays a crucial part in the biblical scheme. Not because they are intended to be the only ones witnessing (as often happens), but because it is their calling to equip the saints for the work of service (Eph. 4:12). Don't let your fear that your people will leave the evangelism to you deter you from a bold and visible witness before them. Lead them by your life and example, and patiently remind them that your work is intended as a *beginning* to a life of corporate witness in the church. This will require consistency, patience, love for your people and a real burden for the lost on your part.

The second point: Sometimes people keep on spreading the gospel when their leaders hold back the message through sluggishness or ignorance, but many stop evangelizing just because their leaders are not doing it. The church is filled to overflowing with examples of this sad chain reaction.

The third point: The Spirit of God lives in every member of Christ's body (I Cor. 12:13), and this Holy One is a witnessing, missionary spirit (John 15:26-27). For this reason evangelistic concern does not completely wither away in the congregation even though the office-bearers evidence little zeal for witness. But when the Spirit kindles a new flame of missionary life, that life may move *outside* the perimeter of the established church. It then comes to maturity without the wisdom of the larger body and the guidance of church leaders.

Ultimately these new forms of missionary life return to the established church as evangelistic organizations or even para-church structures. When this happens, the pastors and elders may find themselves in the awkward position of opposing an evangelistic enterprise which, in spite of doctrinal deficiencies, is obviously being blessed by the Holy Spirit.

In all this there is a healthy jolt for pastors. Has the love of Christ constrained us to be missionary examples to our flocks? Or have we failed to evangelize in our preaching, in our own Sunday school, and in our neighborhood? Do our people breathe in from us a spirit of holy compassion for lost souls, or do they breathe in a spirit of ease in Zion and myopic indifference to the hell which awaits unsaved sinners?

Defining the Example

How can you as a pastor recover the New Testament model for witness? How can you begin to set an example for witness that the whole church will follow? Think for a moment of the biblical descriptions of the pastor to see what God would have you be.

You are a steward, having in your hands God's message and discipline, the keys to the kingdom. You are a herald and ambassador, bringing the good news of salvation from the King. You are an elder-bishop, an under-shepherd, feeding and ruling over the flock in Christ's name, guided by the Word of God. You are also a teacher, expounding the Scriptures, exhorting, warning and rebuking, all in relationship to sound doctrine in the Lord Jesus.

But be warned. If you think of yourself exclusively in those terms, you will very likely come across to men as a lord rather than as a helper for their joy (II Cor. 1:24). In the New Testament the pastor is defined also as a *servant* and *brother* (John 13:1; I Cor. 1:1; II Cor. 1:1; Phil. 2:25). From Christ the elect servant and elder brother, the pastor learns to humble himself in love among the people as *their* servant and brother.

Try to teach and lead the people of God without this identification and you will ring vaguely hollow to them. They will not readily follow you. But take a towel in your hand and wash their feet, and they will see Christ in you. Your example of Christ-like concern will be the model they need to become burdened themselves by the needs of others. Having received a measure of the love of Christ through you, they will be more able to extend it to those around them.

Suppose, for example, a Christian family is troubled by serious conflict between father and son. With patience and loving confrontation, you labor to bring them to shed old patterns of communication and put on Christian ways.

They are grateful and respond to the invitation to go witnessing with you. This emphasis on sharing Christ may sound premature since their problems are not fully resolved, but it has great therapeutic value because it begins to shift emphasis away from themselves to Christ and His kingdom.

Thus, your evangelism will, as James Kennedy has taught us, be caught as well as taught.[2] Unfortunately, however, many pastors spend so little time with their people that the real man—

---

2. Presbyterian scholars as a rule have been slow to appreciate the magnitude of D. James Kennedy's pioneer work as expressed in his *Evangelism Explosion* (Wheaton, Illinois: Tyndale House Publishers, 1970). One of Kennedy's breakthroughs has been to point out that the New Testament presents the pastor as model and trainer who imparts knowledge on the job.

and whatever concern he has for his sheep and the lost—is concealed behind a screen of distant professionalism. It certainly wasn't so with the Apostle Paul. Writing to the Thessalonian church, he notes that he was *gentle among them*, like a father and a nurse (I Thess. 2:7, 11). He also mentions what he assumes they already know: he was not only ready to share the gospel with them, but also to give his life.

The remarkable thing is that nobody laughed. My guess is that if some of today's pastors stood before their congregations and made that announcement, smiling skepticism—at the very least—would be the response! How would your congregation react to such a declaration? Perhaps you are one who must admit that you give your people little to model themselves after. It is therefore not surprising that they lack the zeal and effectiveness of the Thessalonian church's evangelism—their pastor lacks the vision and fervor of the Apostle Paul.

The pastor functioning as a servant and brother knows that *work* is the operative word for his calling: the pastor is a *working* model for his people. Like Epaphroditus he may be called to labor in self-giving right to the door of death (Phil. 2:28-30), to study diligently as a scribe of the kingdom (Matt. 13:52; II Tim. 2:15), and to agonize in prayer for men (Col. 2:1-3; 4:12-13).

On a daily basis, this means that self-indulgence must be put to death in the pastor. Self-indulgence represents a special and continuing temptation to the pastor because his time is largely in his own hands. It takes the form of physical laziness and sluggishness of spirit, which readily fosters fear. Personal timidity and physical exhaustion often seem to issue from the poisoned conscience of the slothful man.

It works like this: the pastor neglects his calling in the community, grows weary of study and finds his preaching and teaching a burden. He also thinks he needs more sleep. And his fear of people grows.

Other sins soon spin out of his disobedient life. Legalistic penance, wheel-spinning, the aggressive pushing of secondary causes in the church, the neglect of matters of first importance—he indulges in it all.

To be rid of this burden of self-indulgence, go to Christ, the perfect Advocate with the Father (I John 2:1-2). By faith hand the sins over to Him. Be specific as you confess your transgressions, and then trust in His forgiveness. He promises it (I John 1:8-10).

If this does not bring fundamental help, ask your elders to pray for you, acknowledging your tendency to self-indulgence. At the same time, ask the Lord to search out your heart for related sins, such as daydreaming and fantasizing.

What you may learn is that the pride that keeps you daydreaming is the fundamental cause of your laziness. You may have been too proud to let the Lord search you and root out your pet sins, whatever they were.

But be comforted. The Holy Spirit will help you (Ps. 139: 23, 24). Christ will write the Father's laws and love on your heart (Ezek. 36:24-25; I Thess. 3:5). And remember, repentance is normal for the believer, his way of responding to Christ and drawing near to the Father (Luke 15:20-24).

Sincere and swift repentance of sinful habits and attitudes can transform the ministry of the most discouraged, ineffectual pastor. Imagine for a moment a young minister who arrives at his study late, already feeling guilty because he has not begun the day in earnest prayer. Usually, the despair produced by habitual sins like these causes him to fritter away his entire time. But today he faces his sins head on. He begins his time by looking to Christ for help. He labors in prayer until he has experienced His cleansing and then seeks God's wisdom in preparing his Sunday sermon (James 1:5-8).

This time, his preparation does not consist solely of an exegesis of the passage and the writing of the sermon text. Instead, the pastor relates his calling as servant and brother to his preaching. He makes a list of several people who concern him, people he suspects may be unconverted or believers with special needs. He then takes time to pray for them.

Afterwards, he returns to the shaping of the sermon in view of the needs of the men and women for whom he has just prayed. He gives up his academic vocabulary and the elements of bookish didacticism as he thinks of their souls. Illustrations come to mind as he mentally reasons from Scripture with these lost and straying sheep. With eyes of faith he sees them—and he will have their souls for God!

By the time he leaves his study, he cannot wait until Sunday to preach. That afternoon, he calls on these people to minister to them in their homes. He is becoming a man who preaches the Word in season and out, and his pulpit and his study are fused into a continuum: in the study he drinks of the gospel as a thirsty sinner, and in the pulpit he pours forth the overflow to other sinners like himself (John 7:37-39).

This pastor is on his way to becoming, like Paul, a model for witness to his people. He begins by seeking the knowledge of Christ from Scripture, a knowledge which so fills him with the love of God that old sins and habits are displaced by a new fulness. Though lazy and filled with fears, he brought both failings to Christ, seeking the strengthening of his faith.

This is the key: strengthening the Christian leader by faith. "The just shall live by faith" must include the pastor's whole life, for it is this that enables him to concentrate his energies, define goals, repent of sins and honestly face up to his own limitations. It is this that makes him a fruit-bearing disciple, eager to have answers to prayer through his own preaching, to have lives come under the power of the gospel. He is not content with a vague concept of "edification"—he prays for his hearers to be brought to a full knowledge of the Father and the Son (John 17:3). And by dealing with his own sins of pride, fear, laziness and lust, he is able to make the message powerfully concrete.

The pastor whom God has made a model for witness is one whose character is inseparably intertwined with his faith in the gospel message. If he did not have confidence in its power to change him, the awareness of his own sins would crush his ministry. But as he leaves his idols to serve Christ, he discovers that the message purifies his heart through faith, and liberates him from all his guilty fears (II Cor. 3:16-18; I Thess. 1:9-10; John 3:1-3). He is a man set free to serve a living God.

CHAPTER EIGHT

How to Involve Your Church
In Evangelistic Outreach

We have seen that visible models for witness are what most churches need before they can evangelize effectively. The pastor must move among his people as a shepherd who cares for them. He must let them see him witness to others. This does not mean that he must do all the work himself—not at all. But the people need to hear him present the gospel with all wisdom, fervor, and boldness.

The next step is to initiate a program involving the congregation in evangelistic outreach themselves. One that fits naturally into most church situations is one that is keyed to family hospitality and natural friendships. It can begin with a broad-based effort at friendship evangelism, in which all the families in the church are encouraged to use their homes to reach out to non-Christians. From there it is a logical step for the pastor to select the more gifted and interested evangelists for further training in witnessing. These persons will be involved in a more structured evangelistic outreach, including systematic calling and a large group evangelistic meeting, which could be repeated and expanded as concern for evangelism grows in the church.

This training class should be taught by someone gifted by the Spirit of God for evangelism. It may be the pastor, it may be a lay leader whose zeal for the lost has been amply demonstrated. Before you actually begin, however, you need to make a realistic assessment of the number of trainees you can handle effectively. Do you have more than one trainer in the church? You need enough experienced people to accompany the trainees on their evangelistic appointments, especially during the early part of the program.

Perhaps you are the only one equipped to be a trainer the first time around. You may conclude that you have the resources and time to work with only one person. Don't be discouraged. It is better to choose one person who has potential as a trainer and to train him well. By so doing, you have doubled your resources. Plan to go through the course three times a year at the beginning. You'll be increasing the number of potential trainers each time around.

At the outset, the trainees should be prepared to commit themselves to one evening of group instruction per week, plus additional time (determined by the pastor or the class) for visitation and for planning the evangelistic meeting. Stress the need for consistent participation to all in the program. Otherwise the entire group loses its enthusiasm and direction because of the thoughtlessness of one or two.

The training program climaxes with a special evangelistic program. This friendship meeting can center upon a ladies' tea, a prayer breakfast, a film, an open house, testimonies at a fish fry, or a discussion group. Its planning should begin early and include others besides those enrolled in the training course. If you are showing a film, the entire church should be invited to come and bring guests, help with refreshments, etc. But the specific planning needs to be done by those being trained. Their task is to bring as many of their evangelistic contacts as possible to the special meeting. This means getting out invitations to new people as soon as possible, though without forcing the issue. It also means supplying transportation for those who need it.

One note of caution: as you develop this program and introduce it to members of your church, be careful to place it in the context of the church's broader life of witness, and the responsibility of each member to be sharing what God has done for him. You want to avoid the impression that participation in this program will fulfill one's evangelistic obligations for the next 10 years! Nevertheless, this program can be helpful when presented as an introduction to organized evangelism and as a training program to equip believers to fulfill their several evangelistic responsibilities. It is an effort to heighten, systematize and deepen what should be taking place in the local congregation.

Organizing the Evangelistic Outreach

The First Step—Prayer: The first step is to get as many people as possible praying for this outreach before it begins. The preaching that you as pastor will do in connection with it, the individuals recruited for training, the unsaved to be contacted, and the congregation's attitude toward the outreach all need to be brought frequently and earnestly to the throne of grace if you would see God's blessing.

Start by cultivating those noble people, the believing aged, and shut-ins. Often they have been well trained already by the great High Priest Himself in the art of intercession. To encourage their effective prayer, be precise in explaining your goals, methods, and problems. Make your prayer requests specific, and let them know promptly what answers have been forthcoming.

Do the same at your elders' meetings. Study Acts 1—9 to show how group prayer was the basis for all church activity after the Lord's resurrection. Ask that a significant part of each official elders' meeting be devoted to prayer, including prayer for the goals of the evangelism program.

Focus portions of the midweek prayer meeting on this same program. Often people do not go to prayer meeting because they do not see its importance or purpose, an attitude frequently confirmed by the widespread use of the hour as a time for Bible study instead of prayer.

Save the long Bible study for another occasion. Instead, make the Bible central in prayer meeting by following its directives for praising God and by using its promises as a basis for intercession. In prayer relate the promises of Scripture to clearly defined needs in the body, including the new emphasis on outreach.

As you do this, seek out interested people to form small prayer groups for this ministry. These groups should meet regularly and, like the other prayer warriors, should be well informed at each phase of the program.

The Second Step—Faith and Hospitality: The second step is to initiate a series of sermons on faith and hospitality. Note the combination—they must go together. Faith without hospitality withers in a vacuum of lovelessness and inactivity; hospitality without ardent faith is merely sociability, lacking the daring purpose of winning souls to King Jesus. But keep the two together, and you have a strategy blessed by God for communicating the gospel.

After the first step of praying has begun in earnest, preach three or four sermons on witness and hospitality, and conclude with a specific challenge on the use of the home in leading friends and neighbors to Christ. One evangelistic organization recommends that each family set itself an annual goal of forming a friendship with one non-Christian and winning him for Christ. Such a specific challenge provides a reasonable minimum standard for every family in the church. Some will do much more, but anyone who knows Christ at all can make one close friend in a year's time.

If this challenge is to be meaningful, however, it must not be contradicted by the example of your own home. As pastor-model, you are required by Scripture to be hospitable (I Tim. 3:2; Titus 1:8). This is your duty and calling simply as a Christian (Heb. 13:2). Therefore, don't be taken in by the old wives' tale that pastors and their spouses cannot make personal friends. You need to explain your goals in this area to God's people and be careful not to commit the sin of partiality, but there is little justification for the notion that you should remain isolated from mankind.

The Third Step—Recruit the Gifted for Further Training: Be on the alert for the individuals who have evidenced real zeal and effectiveness in the use of their homes for witness, and ask them to take part in systematic evangelism training. There is an important spiritual principle at work here. Leadership is not arbitrarily drawn from the top; it rises as the Spirit's gifts of faith are exercised by the body of believers. Your role is that of spiritual midwife: as you assist various families in opening their homes and Bibles to friends, you seek to identify those who are being especially used by God. Ordinarily, this indicates that God is calling them to further training. Do not neglect the rest of the congregation, but for training purposes concentrate your energies here.

Begin by strengthening their faith in the power of the gospel. Give them copies of Spurgeon's *The Passion and Death of Christ*[1] and A. W. Pink's *Profiting from the Word*.[2] Spurgeon captures the power of the cross, and Pink teaches how to apply the Word to yourself with a healthy vigor. Next, show your recruits how to study the Bible, with an emphasis on personal application. Encourage them to meditate on a single chapter like Luke 6 for a month until life changes are seen in the home. Tie this to instruction on the value and power of continued confession of sin and to teaching on the importance of moment-by-moment reliance on the Holy Spirit for deepening obedience and opportunities for witness. Finally, ask them to commit themselves to training and outreach for a period of 10 weeks as a minimum. An agreement to do this is important if the training is to be of any benefit to the trainees.

The Fourth Step—Systematic Calling: This phase should begin six months after your families have begun practicing

---

1. Charles Haddon Spurgeon, *The Passion and Death of Christ* (Grand Rapids: William B. Eerdmans Publishing Co., 1970).

2. Arthur W. Pink, *Profiting from the Word* (London: Banner of Truth Trust, 1970).

evangelistic hospitality in their homes. It involves the setting up of an instruction class composed of the committed recruits you have selected, and the actual process of systematic calling on friends and neighbors (ideally, non-Christians who have experienced Christian hospitality). The first time around, two or three trainees are plenty if you do not have a supply of trainers on hand, since your students will need an experienced person to make calls with them.

If you wish, you can wait for a month before you take out class members for systematic visiting. My own instinct is to whet their appetites by taking them out right away, even though they are not yet prepared to say much. They will learn a great deal by watching you. The program outline in the next chapter sets forth the training schedule in more detail.

You want those being trained to memorize a minimum of three verses a week for the duration of the course. These verses should be chosen to deal with the holiness and love of God, the person and work of Christ, the new birth, repentance, faith, justification, sanctification, the free offer of the gospel, and the authority of Scripture.

During this training period a major goal is to equip the student with the ability to present the gospel in a simple, clear, and natural way. This requires that the pastor not insist on overloading his trainees with numerous evangelistic methods. Certainly, flexibility is a great thing, and pastors should have many evangelistic approaches. But you have years of training and experience that your students do not, so don't expect them to imitate your flexibility at this point.

Choose a method of presenting the gospel that is easily transferable. (The method set forth in these materials is that of the booklet ''A New Life.'') You need a bread-and-butter approach for the beginning evangelist. You can add the jam later.

During this training period you are to give instruction on the nature of the gospel and the law of God. Ask each student to write a three-minute testimony stating the main facts of the way to salvation. Have him commit this to memory and encourage him to share it right away. The governing principles are: (1) Share now and (2) share with the people nearest to you. Begin also to take the student with you to share his testimony during your pastoral calls.

Help in formulating the testimony can be found in D. James Kennedy's *Evangelism Explosion*.[3] Let the emphasis fall on three things: (1) Identification of the witness as formerly self-righteous or unfulfilled, as well as blind to the love of God revealed in Christ; (2) the practical changes the gospel has brought into the life (Gal. 5:22), and the assurance of eternal life (John 3:36); and (3) praise to God for sending His Son to die for such a sinner as yourself.

Step Five—The Evangelistic Evening: The fifth step is a special evangelistic program planned by the trainees and held near the close of the training program. The entire church family should be encouraged to be involved in this informal witness to non-Christian contacts. The key to the success of the program is a Spirit-imparted joy and natural-ness in welcoming people. Concentrate your prayers on this goal and then determine by God's grace to have a good time yourself. Be serious about God's gospel but not grim. And do not be afraid of a touch of class if this is appropriate! Plan something that is really attractive: a film, a winsome speaker on an interesting topic, a mix of fun and games followed by testimonies and refreshments, or a program of music wisely adapted to the audience.

How should you as pastor prepare yourself for the train-ing sessions? The most basic preparation is a spiritual immersion in the Gospel of John. You need to look at Christ through this gospel, seeing the wonder of His person and appropriating for yourself the fulness of His life. You must

---

3. D. James Kennedy, *Evangelism Explosion* (Wheaton, Illinois: Tyndale Publishers, 1970).

not merely adopt the point of view taken in the gospel (which emphasizes the tremendous scope of the Savior's work); you must also be personally caught up in the overflowing new life which streams from Christ.

For my part, I know of no more eloquent treatment of this theme than John Calvin's exposition of John 1:14-18 in his commentary on this Gospel.[4] The commentaries of John by Leon Morris[5] and William Hendriksen[6] are also highly useful. But the best resource is the Gospel of John itself. Therefore, begin your meditation by studying the signs in the Gospel: they all focus on Christ's greatness and vital power shared with the needy through an appropriating faith.

Take as an example Christ's first miracle of turning water into wine: He does not do it on a meager scale. At a time when the wedding is nearing an end, He supplies a superabundance of the best; not to encourage drunkenness but to serve as a sign of the abundant grace available to sinners who drink of Him.

The same message is conveyed by the abundance of bread supplied to the hungry (chap. 6), the healing of the man born blind (chap. 9), and the raising of Lazarus (chap. 11). In each instance, the presence of Christ as the giver of life and light is made powerfully central by the miraculous deed. Man's response is meant to be one of immediate and total appropriation. It is this response you need to ask the Father to awaken in you; it is this response you seek to arouse in your students, and they in those to whom they witness.

4. John Calvin, *Calvin's Commentaries, The Gospel According to St. John*, trans. T. H. L. Parker, vols. I-II (Grand Rapids: William B. Eerdmans Publishing Co., 1959, 1961).

5. Leon Morris, *The New International Commentary, The Gospel According to John* (Grand Rapids: William B. Eerdmans Publishing Co., 1971).

6. William Hendriksen, *New Testament Commentary, Exposition of the Gospel of John* (Grand Rapids: Baker Book House, 1961).

CHAPTER NINE

An Outline for Evangelism Training

This chapter contains the outline for the evangelistic training program described in the previous chapter. This 10-week course, part of a broader evangelistic outreach involving the entire congregation, is designed to train for witness Christians who have not had formal Bible or seminary training. However, since it is also common for those with formal education in the Scriptures to have missed some of the ABC's of effective evangelism, this approach can serve their needs as well.

I call the approach "friendship evangelism" because of the stress upon friendship and deeds of kindness as a foundation for witness (Matt. 5:13-16). Those participating in the training program have already demonstrated a concern for the lost by showing hospitality to them in their homes. The goal here is to seek to bring the good news to men within a framework of demonstrated Christian love. This means that a large part of this outreach strategy involves instructing those participating on the evangelistic opportunities that lie in all their contacts with people, in connection with the church or elsewhere: the deacon in his care for the sick, the poor, the aged, and the dying; the Sunday school teacher opening his home for his students and their families; the youth worker visiting the families of his young people; the businessman opening his life and home to his associates; and the housewife seeking out and welcoming neighbors into her home.

The training program also includes visitation evangelism,

with door-to-door calling and appointments with other contacts. Even this is oriented toward the demonstration of Christ's love wherever possible. If sickness or other need is encountered in the home, those visiting should take appropriate steps to help in any way possible.

Some notes on the large group evangelistic program called for in the course of training are in order here. The key to such a program is to be natural, and to put people together in a setting they can relate to without embarrassment. The evangelistic tea on a weekday morning is a natural situation for women but not for men. Women find it normal to be invited to a neightbor's home for tea or coffee. And given the added inducement of a distinguished speaker treating a relevant topic on a popular level, they are likely to respond favorably to such an invitation. One theme that has drawn goodly numbers has been surprisingly direct: "How Jesus Christ Can Help You Be a Better Wife and Mother."

For men, the monthly or bimonthly Saturday morning prayer breakfast has proved to be attractive. Such an event consists of a rather early morning breakfast, followed by brief prayer and a well-known speaker in a church hall or local restaurant. Again, a theme that has brought positive response has been: "How Jesus Christ Can Help You Be a Better Husband and Father." The speaker must be carefully chosen. He needs some understanding of middle-class men, if that is his audience, and an ability to establish rapport with them while sharing the gospel in a winsome, practical manner. It is also important that the speaker be a man of faith and prayer in order that the Spirit of God bless this undertaking.

At evening meetings, a dinner followed by a film like "The Conversion of Colonel Bottomley" puts unbelievers at ease and yet brings into sharp focus how Christ saved a highly typical, hard-driving American man. The secret of such a meeting is to avoid hymns and the extensive use of Christian vocabulary which frightens or alienates non-Christians. Open with a simple prayer and arrange to have after the film an informal discussion

71

of what it means to know Christ. Of course, it would be even better to have your people discuss the film with your guests on a one-to-one basis, giving the unbelievers an opportunity to respond in a casual manner.

More difficult but sometimes spectacularly effective is a discussion group format like that run by Mr. and Mrs. Bertrand Alpers in Pipersville, Pennsylvania. As new converts, they modeled their outreach along the lines of their former cocktail party encounters. Biweekly meetings were held on Friday evenings, with guests receiving a formal invitation to each affair. The invitations included a catchy statement of the subject to be discussed, which is anything from "What is a Religious Fanatic?" to "The Happiest Day of My Life Was. . . ."

When the guests arrived, they were given pencil and paper and asked to write their reponse to the evening's topic. The unsigned answers were dropped into a bowl, mixed up, and then taken from the bowl and read one by one by the couple's pastor. Some were amusing, others serious. Afterwards, the minister briefly read the answer the Bible supplies to the question. Refreshments followed and the discussion continued, often beginning to break open around midnight. Typically, the last guest would leave around 3:00 A.M. Any number of conversions resulted from these casual dialogues.

A progressive dinner can also be highly effective because it is an easy way to involve a number of neighbors. But if you plan to conclude with a gospel presentation, keep it muted in tone, and let the neighbors know from the outset that you will have testimonies at some point, so that they are not left feeling that you tricked them into participating. A fish fry or barbecue also provides an appropriate setting for two or three carefully chosen testimonies to bring the evening to a climax.

(Note: On the following course outline, the chapters listed in parentheses after each "Theme" under the Weekly Instruction Period refer to the chapters in this book which deal with the topic to be discussed.)

TEN WEEK EVANGELISTIC TRAINING
PROGRAM

WEEK ONE:
Memory Work
John 10:10; Gal. 5:22, 23

Weekly Assignment
Reading: Ps. 67; Luke 8:26-39; Acts 8:1-8; Acts 16:1-40

Weekly Instruction Period One and One Half Hours
1. Getting to know one another
2. Program introduction
3. Questions answered and assignments made
4. Theme: "How to Witness Through Deeds of Kindness" (chaps. 6, 8)

Outreach by Word and Deed
1. Trainer leads, arranges appointments with trainee to visitors, neighbors, other contacts.
2. Trainee does deed of kindness to at least one neighbor and seeks to use it as basis for honoring Christ. Keep it simple.

WEEK TWO:
Memory Work
John 3:16; Rom. 1:16; Rom. 3:23

Weekly Assignment
Write 3-minute testimony emphasizing knowing Christ by faith alone (chap. 8).

Weekly Instruction Period One and One Half Hours
1. Theme: "How to Talk about the Love and Power of God" (chaps. 1—3)
2. Share experiences and 3-minute testimonies.
3. Introduce booklet "A New Life"—Fact One.
4. Begin plans for evangelistic program: date, location, speaker, format.

Outreach by Word and Deed
1. Trainer leads, arranges appointments.
2. Trainee opens home to friend or neighbor: hospitality evangelism via dinner or coffee.

WEEK THREE:
Memory Work
Eph. 2:1, 8–9

Weekly Assignment
Improve 3-minute testimony. Read half of *How to Give Away Your Faith* (Paul Little).[1]

Weekly Instruction Period One and One Half Hours
1. Theme: "How to Present the Nature of Sin from God's Point of View"—Facts two and three of New Life booklet (chap. 3)
2. Role playing—going through booklet
3. Begin guest list for evangelistic program, plan refreshments, etc.

Outreach by Word and Deed
1. Trainer leads, arranges appointments.
2. Trainee pursues previous friendship contacts and visits nursing home, with or without trainer.

WEEK FOUR:
Memory Work
Jer. 17:9; John 8:34; Heb. 7:26

Weekly Assignment
Write 2-minute Christ-centered interpretation of a deed of kindness (week no. 1) as a means to use witness of deed as lead-in for witness of word.

Weekly Instruction Period One and One Half Hours
1. Theme: "How Christ Breaks the Barriers Between God and Man"—Fact Four of New Life booklet (chaps. 3, 4)

---

1. Paul Little, *How to Give Away Your Faith* (Chicago: Intervarsity Press, 1966).

2. Role playing with New Life booklet

Outreach by Word and Deed
1. Trainer leads door-to-door calling; trainee gives testimony.
2. Trainee follows up previous friendship contacts and makes new ones.

WEEK FIVE:
Memory Work
Ezek. 36:25−26; Col. 1:13

Weekly Assignment
Read second half of *How to Give Away Your Faith*.

Weekly Instruction Period One and One Half Hours
1. Theme: ''How to Lead a Person to Christ: the nature of faith and repentance''—Fact Five of New Life booklet (chap. 12)
2. Share visitation experiences.
3. Emphasize faith and repentance of trainee.

Outreach by Word and Deed
1. Same as previous week
2. Prepare list of names and addresses of those to be invited to evangelistic program.

WEEK SIX:
Memory Work
Acts 16:31; Isa. 55:7; I John 1:9

Weekly Assignment
Read Ps. 51 and Luke 15. Study Westminster Confession and Shorter Catechism on saving faith and repentance to life.

Weekly Instruction Period One and One Half Hours
1. Test on memory verses
2. Theme: ''How to Help New Christians Grow in their Knowledge of God's Love and Forgiveness'' (chap. 4)

Outreach by Word and Deed
1. Trainee takes lead. Trainer gives testimony. Trainee makes appointments.
2. Mail invitations to evangelistic program.

WEEK SEVEN:
Memory Work
John 15:16; Eph. 1:4; Ezek. 33:11

Weekly Assignment
Read Charles Spurgeon's "Election"[2] or R.B. Kuiper's *God-Centered Evangelism,* chapter 3.[3]

Weekly Instruction Period One and One Half Hours
1. Test on use of New Life booklet
2. Theme: "God's Sovereignty as the Basis for Evangelism" (chaps. 1, 2, 11)

Outreach by Word and Deed
1. Trainee makes appointments, takes lead, pursues previous contacts, invites new contacts to evangelistic program.

WEEK EIGHT:
Memory Work
Matt. 11:28; John 7:37−38

Weekly Assignments
Read John 3, 4, 9 and Luke 7:36−50

Weekly Instruction Period One and One Half Hours
1. Theme: "How to Use Natural Ways to Introduce the Gospel to Men" (chaps. 8, 9)
2. Role-playing: Guiding the conversation to Christ

Outreach by Word and Deed
1. Continue follow-up or seek new contacts.
2. Finalize all plans for evangelistic program.

WEEK NINE:
Memory Work
John 15:7−8; Matt. 18:19

2. Charles Haddon Spurgeon, "Election" (Philadelphia: Great Commissions Publications, n.d).
3. R.B. Kuiper *God-Centered Evangelism: A Presentation of the Scriptural Theology of Evangelism* (Grand Rapids: Baker Book House, 1961).

Weekly Assignments
Read John 15 and E.M. Bounds' "Power through Prayer."[4]

Weekly Instruction Period One and One Half Hours
1. Theme: "How to Pray for Your Evangelistic Outreach" (chap. 5)
2. Discussion: Using the promises of God in prayer, the importance of praise

Outreach by Word and Deed
1. Week for evangelistic program: Phone calls, personal visits to remind those invited to attend
2. Program possiblities: discussion group, party, open house, film

WEEK TEN:
Memory Work
I Pet. 4:12-14

Weekly Assignments
Read I Peter

Weekly Instruction Period One and One Half Hours
1. Evaluation of special program
2. Theme:"How to Teach New Converts to Witness" (chaps. 4, 11, 13, 14)

Outreach by Word and Deed
1. Follow up of evangelistic program contacts.

4. E.M. Bounds *Power Through Prayer* (Grand Rapids: Baker Book House, reprinted 1963).

CHAPTER TEN

Five Steps to a Gracious Evangelistic Encounter

As you have introduced the friendship evangelism program (or some other organized program of outreach) into your church, you may have found people surprisingly willing to open their homes to non-Christians. A promising group may be prepared to take further training in evangelistic methods. But nearly all those involved (not to mention those who aren't) express concern about their ability to present the gospel calmly, clearly, and completely to their listeners. They have many unresolved fears about their ability to communicate the Christian message.

As pastor, you need first to remind them that "the battle is not yours, but God's" (II Chron. 20:15). The Holy Spirit has been given them to guide them into all wisdom and to enable them to speak the word with clarity. You might also remind them that the best way to build up confidence and expertise in communicating is by talking to people! The five basic principles of presentation which follow should provide your people with a general understanding of how to share their faith.

1. The first principle in effective evangelism is to preach as much of the gospel as you can without confusing or overloading the mind of the hearer. You want to give an overview of the gospel which provides the principal facts, focusing on a crucified and glorified Savior. It is this fulness of preaching that produces faith in God's elect (Rom. 10:17).

A practical implication is that it is usually better to avoid questions which lead to endless debate. Often the very reason these questions exist is the hearer's ignorance of the whole gospel system. Take the famous (and almost inevitable) question, "What about the heathen in Africa who never heard about Christ?" That question cannot be answered without explaining the whole plan of salvation. If you can get the listener to defer his questions until you have explained the entire message more fully, you will be more effective in convincing him of his own need—which at the moment is far more to the point!

2.   Pray for yourself and recruit others to pray that you will present the gospel with the humble gracious authority of an ambassador of Christ. God must convince you that you have a right to go to men with the gospel. It is not they who are doing you a favor to listen; you are doing them a favor to bring them this soul-transforming message. This is a matter of faith. The devil will really attack you on this point, so guard your heart.

3.   Aim the message at the man and state it in language he can understand. The first principle of effective communication is to know what you intend to communicate and then to find the words to express it. You must develop a simple, expressive vocabulary that pictures for the man the essential gospel truths. There is no better guide than the Scriptures themselves. They are vivid, clear and concrete. Allied to this is the principle of necessary repetition. Expect to repeat the message in at least three different ways during a presentation if you hope to have it understood. Don't take anything for granted. Trust the Holy Spirit to apply the message, but remember that the Holy Spirit usually blesses clear speaking and thinking the most.

4.   In all this, labor to make known the claims of God as Creator. The gospel message is what saves the man; it must have priority, therefore, in the presentation. However, make very clear to men that the law of God reveals that this is no mere projection of man's religious genius. The law shows that man is a dependent being made by God, a creature upon whom the Creator has absolute claim. God is not only man's keeper; He is also man's owner and master. To sin, therefore, is to be unthankful to this Creator-Master, to fight against Him with a

rebellious heart, and to attempt to play God by acting as though the sinner had independent powers of wisdom and strength. For the creature to take such a stand against the Almighty is an act of irrational madness. For this reason, Scripture often relates sin to folly and madness (Prov.; Dan. 4:4; Luke 15:17).

At this point your God-consciousness is of first importance. If you do not have strong convictions about the reality of a sovereign God, the absoluteness and finality of His laws, and your total dependence upon Him, it will be difficult to convince anyone else of God's claims upon them.

5.   Finally, once you have presented the whole system of truth, you must wait for the person who is listening to respond. This is difficult for talkative people to do, or for those with aggressive personalities. But it must be done. You are seeking to keep them from feeling (or actually being) psychologically trapped by a stronger personality. You are waiting for God's truth to sink in. In faith you wait on the Creator to work while you wait for the man to speak. And you are intent on seeing what this man knows about Him. By your listening, you are really giving the man your respect, and, most important, an opportunity to respond to God rather than to you. Here, as throughout your conversation, manners are extremely important. They are the means by which grace is made visible. Remember, the whole purpose of your presentation is to bring the man into the presence of God. And this does not happen if he hears you talking all the time.

CHAPTER ELEVEN

What to Say When Men Say "No"

According to Abraham Kuyper, Reformed preachers have often thought they were preaching the gospel when they were only describing it. Gospel preaching includes an imperative, and the preacher must demand the conversion of his hearers. "To be free from a man's blood," he enjoins us, "we must tell every man that conversion is his urgent duty. . . ."[1]

Keep Kuyper's concerns in mind as you lead your congregation in evangelism, for he has put his finger on a problem characteristic of many Reformed and Presbyterian churches. Pastors tend merely to describe the gospel to their hearers and their people generally follow the pattern. They do not ask friends, neighbors, and their children to come to Christ. After all, they reason, is not man totally depraved and unable to come until wrought upon by the power of God? Why then ask a man to do what he cannot do?

These are good questions and deserve an answer. In fact, they *must* be answered if you hope to carry on an evangelistic outreach with any measure of conviction or power. Earlier we said that the gospel message must be aimed at men directly. Now, consider for whom we speak when approaching men with the truth. We speak for a risen Lord. We come with the royal authority of the resurrected Christ.

The way we present our message needs to reflect its authority.

---

1. Abraham Kuyper, *The Work of the Holy Spirit* (Grand Rapids: William B. Eerdmans Publishing, Co., 1956), p. 353.

Sinners rarely respond to a toothless love. They ordinarily do not see any necessity for coming to the cross until they discover that it is not one option among many. They need to be shown that it is a Lion who calls them to rest on the finished work of the Lamb. As G. Campbell Morgan has pointed out, we preach the gospel of the cross from the standpoint of the risen and sovereign Lord of men and history.[2]

Therein lies our justification for a bold, confrontational presentation of the gospel of Christ. Christ the resurrected Lord commands men to repent and believe the gospel as an urgent and solemn duty.

The lordship of Christ also enables us to deal with the issue of human inability in a biblical way. Often I have heard ministers and seminary students describing inability in such a way that the unbeliever is given an excellent excuse for rejecting the message.

These evangelists are readily silenced when a man says of their exposition of the gospel, "You are right. I never thought of it before, but I can see that I am totally depraved and unable to change myself. But why get so excited? It's unfair to expect me to do anything about it. If I must die in my sins then at least I can go on and enjoy them while I live."

Such an objection shows a sinful blindness to the actual nature of human inability. It is quite true that God's sovereign grace must work first if men are to be converted. The power to turn must come from God. Because of the corruption of the human heart, men cannot by their own strength find God or even prepare themselves to do so (Gen. 6:5; 8:21; Jer. 17:9; Matt. 15:19; John 1:13; 6:37, 44; Eph. 2:1-4). But it is of crucial significance to see the particular nature of man's inability. Man's *cannot* is shot through with a moral *will not*. It is not that man is a good fellow who would *like* to turn to God but is prevented from doing so by some external force alien to his human nature. Man rejects Christ because his will, his heart,

2. G. Campbell Morgan, *Evangelism* (Worthing & London: Henry E. Walter Ltd., 1964), pp. 7-24.

and his disposition are set against the Lord. Here we see the breaking of the first commandment and man's willful rejection of God's way. "All we like sheep have gone astray, and we have turned every one to his own way" (Isa. 53:6). He loves his own way and not God's service. Regrettably, his innate and inexcusable desire is to yield himself to the service of unrighteousness (Rom. 6:16-18).

Our evangelism must make it clear to the sinner that this is what is happening in his life. He dare not think that his lost condition is not his concern. Nor must his inability to save himself be permitted to become a refined excuse for a stubborn refusal to come to Christ. This is why Paul reminds the Romans that knowing Christ is no great superhuman activity. We do not need to ascend to the heavens to get Him or descend to the deep to bring Him up (Rom. 10:6-8). Instead, the word of faith brought by the preacher is on our lips and in our hearts. We simply yield ourselves in trust, believing that God raised Him up from the dead, confessing this with our mouths, and we are saved (Rom. 10:9).

The lordship of Christ means that men are utterly without excuse. As the Canons of Dort note, "Men do not perish for want of an atonement." Nor must we permit them to perish without a warning.

Remember this when you are preaching, witnessing or using the "New Life" booklet. Christ's sovereignty does not mean that we are free to force the booklet on people, but it does mean that we have a right to approach men in such a way that they are made aware that the crucified Christ is now the living Lord of glory. This living Lord expects men to bow to His person and His Word. Therefore we must expect them to respond as we rely on His Spirit to accomplish this in the lives of many.

CHAPTER TWELVE

How to Witness with the "New Life" Booklet

Because of abuses both real and imagined, many Christians have little use for tracts and "witnessing booklets." In particular, they fear a mechanical approach to the Christian witness which minimizes personal contact from man to man. They also rightly suspect that brief written summaries can truncate the gospel or be used to bring about hasty "decisions" that have nothing in common with biblical conversion.

These dangers are real enough. But they can be avoided by careful submission to the principles found in the Word of God. When this submission governs our approach, we discover that written materials are greatly used of God in clarifying the gospel, first for ourselves, and then for those to whom we speak. If properly developed, such evangelistic instruments can provide a comprehensive picture of the Christian faith, an overview introducing non-Christians to the broad sweep of Christian teaching. This has great advantages because many unbelievers have completely erroneous conceptions of the Christian faith.

Likewise, such presentations help witnessing Christians to see Bible doctrines from the standpoint of Scripture's evangelical center. They balance the Christian by almost forcing him to subjugate his own "pet" doctrines to the presentation of the gospel as a whole. One man may tend to focus on sin and the law of God, another on Christ and God's mercy, and yet another on the conversion experience. All this is fine, but we must not make one aspect of truth the whole truth, especially when we present the gospel.

Within Reformed circles this need for balance is especially pressing. Our recent history has been all too often one of reaction against Arminianism and semi-Arminianism. As a consequence, many Reformed pastors have virtually dropped the preaching of the cross from their pulpit ministry. And Reformed people as a whole hesitate to tell men about the death of Christ for fear of falling into a man-centered approach to the lost.

I am convinced that a witnessing guide based upon sound biblical theology can avoid the dangers described and help Christians to offer a God-centered presentation of the gospel to the lost. Not the least of its value is the fact that a well-written tract can also function as an icebreaker, a natural way to get into a serious conversation about very personal matters. This is especially important because some Christians just do not know how to engage unbelievers in conversation about the things of Christ.

A tract or booklet does not need to be thrown at strangers like a hand grenade into an enemy camp. One person wisely noted that it functions best as an extension of your arm. It is a tool to be used in a highly personal way—warmly, graciously, and wisely, with complete reliance on the Holy Spirit.

It is for such use that the booklet "A New Life" has been prepared.[1] Its stress falls on the Christian message as the personal gospel of hope for men trapped in their sins and miseries. Without in any way compromising the particularity of Christ's atonement, the booklet emphasizes the personal love of God for sinners, the availability of grace for men in their lost condition, and the power of the gospel to meet them where they are.

What follows is an outline of the "New Life" booklet to help the Christian develop a detailed understanding of the way it presents the gospel. Familiarity with its structure will greatly enhance a free and natural presentation.

Jesus' method of witnessing in John 4 provides the basic

---

1. See appendix.

outline for the booklet. He begins by calling attention to Himself as the gift of God, the source of a supernatural life for man (John 4:10, 14). Afterwards He speaks to the woman about her sins in a very particular way (vss. 16-18). But He focuses first on the grace of God, and only within this context does He draw attention to the law of God.

Here the gospel of hope provides the controlling framework, and the doctrine of man's sin is presented within this particular structure. Condemnation thus can be of the severest sort when properly related to the gospel message. But exposure of sin apart from God's mercy rarely brings sinners to repentance.

FACT ONE: A loving God sent His Son Jesus into the world to bring you to a new and abundant life.

There are two aims here. First, the intention is to show that God's purpose toward the world is to save it. The world is already under condemnation because of its unbelief, but Jesus has been sent by the Father to save.

Hence, God's purpose in the gospel is positive (John 3:17; I Tim. 1:15). It is good news for those who of themselves deserve only the bad news of eternal wrath.

Secondly, the intention is to stress the power and fulness of Jesus' person and work in dealing with man's sins and miseries. A normal Christian life is one in which empty sinners become full through daily drinking of Christ.

Thus the gospel is a message of hope both in God's saving intention toward sinners, and God's saving power for sinners.

FACT TWO: People are self-centered, not God centered.

Here we introduce the idea of sin in words understandable to contemporary people. It is presented as an attitude, or a state of mind, in rebellion against the Creator. In his rebellion man as a creature centers his life on himself and not on God. This self-centered outlook is called being "dead in trespasses and sins" (Eph. 2:1). It expresses itself in dependent man proclaiming his independence of his Maker. This blindness is named "The Big Lie."

Since this self-centered life contradicts reality, man finds himself and his societies torn by the vicious habits and acts that are described in Romans 1:21-32 and listed on page 7 of the booklet (see appendix p. 114). These outworkings of man's self-deception point him to the deeper cause of his sorrows—his rejection of his dependent creaturehood. What we want him to see is that the root of his problems lies in his denial of the Creator's total claim on him as a creature made in His image. People today are accustomed to taking each religious system as just one more set of interesting opinions, and need to be faced with God's absolute claim on every person as the Owner of all. Man needs to know that God has made him and has a right to call him to repentance for his self-centered life.

FACT THREE: Self-centered man is separated from a Holy God by three big barriers.

Here sin is presented from God's point of view. Three wide barriers of sin—a bad record, a bad heart, and a bad master— separate God and man. God has a holy refusal to meet with man, and man, an unholy refusal to meet with God. That is, a holy God cannot come to man without a removal of the three barriers of man's unholiness. Man refuses to come to God because he loves his sin and hates God.

As a consequence, God has a "problem" with man's sin in that He cannot pardon it without a just basis, a proper ground. It is not a problem in the sense of God's being frustrated or helpless, but He is not free to forgive and cleanse men of sin without a mediator. And man left to himself can only receive the wages of sin which he has earned, namely, eternal death.

FACT FOUR: God's solution! No barriers!

God's solution to the problem of sin is to introduce a perfectly righteous Mediator, Jesus the God-man, who breaks through the three barriers of sin and brings God and man together. His righteousness enables a holy God to justify the ungodly (Rom. 4:5).

Observe carefully that the Lord Jesus supplies everything sinful man lacks, a perfect record for a bad record, a new heart for a bad heart, and Himself as a good master for the bad mastery of sin.

The Son of God accomplishes this by becoming the substitute man, the righteous representative of sinners, who goes to the cross in the place of His people. He dies in the culmination of a life of perfect obedience and service to God. Unrighteous man had earned eternal death, but now a righteous Man earns eternal life for His own sheep and gives it as a free gift to those who believe.

FACT FIVE: How to receive the Lord Jesus into your life. . .

In this section the sinner learns what God expects of him. He is told that he may have salvation *now* by turning from his sins and trusting in Jesus alone as Lord and Savior.

Be careful at this point, for man's natural bent is to center on himself, and he will likely think of his repenting and believing as something he does apart from Christ. This is a grave mistake and produces religious experience that is largely psychological. Therefore stress that repenting and believing is God's appointed way of coming to Christ, and that Christ alone does the saving.

Begin a New Life

In this section, the person going through the booklet is challenged to respond to what he has learned about Christ and God. The prayer is a guideline for the man who wishes to receive Christ, but it must not be presented as a magical guarantee that anyone will be automatically saved by praying it. Afterward, the man should not be given assurance that the mere offering of a prayer saves him.

However, Scripture does promise that whosoever calls upon the name of the Lord will be saved (Rom. 10:13). Therefore the man who sincerely calls upon God to save him using this prayer or his own words will, in fact, find God ready to save him.

Since salvation begins in prayer, the booklet strongly urges upon the new believer the necessity for continuing to pray. Prayer, broadly understood, is resented as the central and distinguishing feature of the Christian life. Bible reading and Bible study are also presented as steps in obedience to the resurrected Lord. The man who has trusted in Jesus has a secret resurrection life (Col. 3:1-4), and it is to be expected that he now has the power from the Lord to put his sins to death (Col. 3:5-11).

The emphasis on worship in a scripturally directed church is combined with a call for meditation on God, His world, and our place in it. The purpose here is to challenge the new disciple to begin to think in a Christian manner about all areas of life and to see his Father's hand in everything that comes to pass.

Encourage the new convert to witness in a natural, kindly way to friends and relatives, remembering that shortly before, he too was blind to the great mercies of God. Especially discourage witnessing in pride and any idea that the disciple has new life or power apart from Christ.

Now you are ready to share the booklet with others. Do you find yourself hesitating? All your friends and neighbors suddenly seem self-sufficient. Why would they want to hear about Christ?

Wait a moment! Don't abandon evangelism before you even begin! Don't try to choose the elect! That happens to be God's task. How do you know whom God will call to Himself? God has a sovereign plan conceived in all wisdom. In that plan He brings you to the people He wants you to meet. Is it not likely that He will be guiding you to His own sheep among your friends? Be a friend with a difference. Be more friendly than you ever were before and prepare yourself to witness by taking the following steps:

1. Pray before you go with the gospel, asking God to prepare both you and the person you meet. Make an essential part of this prayer a specific request for humble, loving boldness. The gospel is a message having God's own authority. If you act and

speak as though you were not a messenger of the great King, then you are a virtual contradiction to what you are saying.

In practical terms, this means you must believe that you have a right to bring the gospel to men. Those who listen to you are not doing you a favor; you, rather, are doing them a favor. Keep this in mind especially when you are discouraged by opposition and conflict.

Develop some natural introductions for presenting the "New Life" booklet. A natural introduction can be very effective when you yourself are enthusiastic about the booklet.

One opening might be: "Have you seen the booklet called 'A New Life'? It's really meant a lot to me, and I'd like to share with you some of the things I've learned from it."

Another might be: "George, you know, a lot of people have been looking at this booklet called 'A New Life.' I have a copy of it here which you can take with you. After you read it, let's get together and talk about it."

Again, "Mary, you said you couldn't believe the Bible. I can understand your problem. But have you ever really gotten an overview of what the whole Bible is about? It certainly wouldn't be fair to yourself or to the Scriptures if you didn't take a little time to consider the central message of the Bible. And you can catch something of the broad picture through a little booklet I have here."

2. Start using the booklet immediately. Simply take your pen and circle the main words and draw arrows to the principal thoughts. At times this will seem absurd and useless. But fight off the thought that this person listening isn't paying attention. Be enthusiastic about Christ's love and tremble as you consider the awfulness of man's sin. You can be sure that most people will listen then.

3. Be thoroughly familiar with the booklet yourself. Memorize the Scriptures cited and study the connections between the various facts. For example, the relationship between facts 1 and 2 is that of contrast. Therefore, emphasize the difference between the new life given by the Spirit as set forth in

Galatians 5:22 and the state of man described in Ephesians 2:1-3.

Facts 3 and 4 are related to each other by way of problem (fact 3) and solution (fact 4). Sin is the problem; Christ is the solution. Bring this out as you go.

Especially note the question at the bottom of page 11 (see appendix p.116). Ask it. Then wait until the person responds. In many instances the person will say that he hopes to be accepted into heaven on the basis of God's general kindness and his own good works. If you get this answer, turn back to facts 3 and 4 and go over the three barriers again, and Christ's work as Mediator in removing them.

Similarly, in going over fact 5, I often find it helpful to turn again to 4 and relate faith to Christ's breaking the barriers.

Try to move through the booklet at a good pace. You can always come back and go through the booklet a second or third time. But I usually try to cover most of the five facts in about 30 minutes. The reason for this rate of speed is to give the person an overview of the whole message in a rather short time, and to keep from getting sidetracked so that the booklet doesn't get covered. (This half hour, of course, does not include the time spent on "How Does This New Life Continue?")

Remember: faith is the motivational force for Christian witness. And you get more faith as you seek it by prayer and earnest Bible study. Thus you go to the work of evangelism with a seriousness and a determination wrought by the Holy Spirit.

However, faith often seems to be at its lowest ebb just before you go forth with the message. Satan may shower the believer at such moments with doubts. But then as you go you are astonished to see how faith and joy begin to abound.

Why? The answer is that God gives the Holy Spirit "to those who obey him" (Acts 5:32), and going with the gospel is one of the many ways that the believer expresses his obedience as a disciple (Matt. 28:16-20; II Cor. 5:20).

And I tell you, everyone who confesses me before men, the Son of man will confess before the angels of God; but he who denies me before men will be denied before the angels of God (Luke 12:8-9).

CHAPTER THIRTEEN

Baptism: The Baby Christian's First Step

To the beginning evangelist, it may seem that no activity could require more prayer and faith than that of witnessing to the lost. But a Christian who has known the joy of seeing a person profess faith in Christ knows that his work is only beginning. The "follow-up" of new converts, as the process of nurture and discipleship has come to be called, is a vital part of any evangelistic ministry. Most popular books on evangelism offer a chapter on the subject somewhere around this point of the book. I would like to deal with the responsibilities of the soul-winner from a slightly different angle, by addressing the responsibilities of the new believer.

Should you have the privilege of leading a person to faith in Christ, it is important that you stress to him that the Holy Spirit's immediate goal for his life is a highly visible public confession of Christ before his family, among his friends, on the job and in the church of God. Think back to our earlier discussion of the Holy Spirit's ministry in the world. His design is to exalt Christ as God's triumphant Son. He has been sent into the world to reveal to men that what appeared to be the scandal of a crucified Jewish criminal is actually the redemptive sacrifice of the Author and Sustainer of the universe. And, as we have also seen earlier, every Christian has a part in declaring this truth.

Leon Morris summarizes the Spirit's work as a commissioning by the Father to vindicate the Son by acting as a friendly prosecuting attorney. In his commentary on John 16:8, he notes: "We have seen that the word translated 'comforter' is a word with legal implications. . . . Normally it denotes a person whose activities are in favor of the defendant. Here, however, the meaning is that the Spirit will act as prosecutor and bring about the world's conviction.''[1]

Seen in the additional light of Acts 2, we can say that this work of the Spirit consists in His presenting the case of the gospel message in the private courtroom of the soul, accusing, softening and turning it to Christ. When the sinner is brought to see the truth of the gospel, he is moved by the Spirit to know, trust and confess Christ as his only hope. His subsequent public confession by testimony and baptism vindicates the cross by the demonstration of its power in his life. It has led him to renounce the world and take on the name of Jesus in this holy ordinance.

Thus in baptism the Spirit's primary goal for the Christian has been realized. It is not that He has no other goals for the new child of God, but He wants this public vindication of Christ's victory to be kept in the forefront. And such an emphasis on baptism and the public confession it involves greatly strengthens an evangelistic ministry. It challenges the unsaved hearer to take neither the love nor the judgment of God lightly, and forces him to deal decisively with his indifference to Christ and/or his fear of ostracism if he becomes a Christian.

The value of an emphasis on early baptism was vividly demonstrated to me in the case of John, a middle-aged husband and father who knew the gospel but never seemed to act upon it. His son suffered a serious eye injury, which provided me an occasion to demonstrate love and concern, and also the chance to talk to John about Christ when his heart was a little softer.

''John, are you familiar with the second commandment?'' asked a friend of mine as the three of us sat together during one visit. A strange look came across John's face. ''That's really something—your talking about *that* commandment. Hardly a day goes by without my thinking about it. I don't want my son and his son to be repeating my sins.''

---

1. Morris, *Gospel According To John*, p. 697.

94

John had the sense of the commandment correctly in its focus on God's jealousy for His own worship and its warning that those who trespass here will see their sins visited on their descendents for three or four generations. We explained that the blood of Christ could not only cancel the guilt of his sin, but also break its hold on his life so that it would not be handed on to his son by way of condemnation.

Using Romans 10:10, I reminded John that he knew the content of the gospel already, but it had never done anything for him. "Isn't the problem that the 'Christ' you know is not a living Lord? Your 'Christ' seems to have died for sins, but He never rose again to the center of power. There is no power in the blood of Christ unless Jesus lives to present the merits of that blood to the Father as the reason for our forgiveness."

John read the passage carefully. "That must be it. I just never took Jesus seriously as the living Lord." Shortly afterwards, he surrendered his life to Christ. In the process, he asked, "You don't expect me to come over to the church and give one of those testimonies, do you?"

I laughed and said, "Yes, and not only that, but Christ expects you to invite your friends and relatives and be baptized at the same time! Christ doesn't want any big speeches. You simply need to share what Jesus' blood now means to you and that Jesus is now your Lord."

John's baptism soon followed and was very instructive to me in the way it delivered the man from some of his key weaknesses. Perhaps most important, it caused him to face Christ publicly and affirm Him as living Lord. It forced him to leave behind his intellectual indifference and allowed him to establish his new identity as a Christian before those who knew him. There really is no easy way for John to turn back to his old life now, and, by all evidences, he is grateful for the opportunity to be publicly aligned and sealed in Christ.

As it did in John's life, this emphasis on baptism goes a long way to solve many of the problems of follow-up. First, it establishes a more biblical perspective for the soul-winner who worries that the perseverance of the new convert rests on his more mature shoulders. Certainly we are responsible to nurture new believers in the Word of God, but it is a great mistake to center our faith on *our* part in the undertaking and not on the power of the Holy Spirit. He is the One who separates the new believer from the world and brings him into fellowship with the body of Christ. Too many Christian leaders have been temporarily (some, permanently) sidelined from the ministry by their anxiety over the struggles and falls of those who profess Christ. We need rather to trust the new believer to the lordship of Christ, as it is displayed in the sovereign might of the Spirit, and as a consequence of his testimony, welcome him as a *confessing* member of the local church. If he begins to backslide, he should be disciplined for purposes of renewal just like any other member.

Secondly, the prospect of an imminent public baptism has a wonderful way of weeding out spurious responses to the gospel. In many communities in America, some knowledge of the gospel is part of the culture, and sinners vaguely sense that they ought to have some kind of "religious experience" to be a complete person. "Decisions" for Christ sometimes spring out of this impulse and not from the conviction of the Spirit. But a decision is far more likely to result in a lifetime commitment when it is expected that the new convert will tell his co-workers and friends about his baptism and invite them to see it take place.

Third, a speedy baptism will help the new Christian to see from the outset that his salvation is not his own work, but part of the ongoing ministry of the Spirit. It puts his eyes not on himself or on the one who led him to Christ, but on the Lord whose Spirit moved him to separate from the world and to take Christ's name upon him. With this foundation, I find that the new convert is much more interested in learning to pray. And that is because his baptism has given him something definite to pray about! Take John, for example, whose story was recounted earlier. He works in an auto repair shop. He resolved to tell each of his co-workers and his boss, who is Jewish, about his baptism and what Christ has done for him. Now he *knows* he needs help! It was not hard at all to get him to see the place of intercessory prayer in his life. In fact, I was not at all surprised that, within a month, John and his wife started a Wednesday night prayer meeting in their home!

It follows from what has already been said that, fourthly, witness by baptism defines from the outset the new believer as a witness. As a church member he is not a passive observer of a liturgical drama, but he is living for Jesus Christ in the church and the world. For him, witnessing is not a "super-natural" extra but an activity tied up with the whole new life and being of the child of God. His instruction for baptism should teach him that he is now indwelt by the Holy Spirit through faith (Gal. 3,4) and that this Holy Spirit of witness can be relied upon completely to enable him to share Christ with the lost (Luke 24: 48-49; Acts 1:8). Given this basis for confidence and the immediate opportunity to see friends or relatives at his public confession, he is very likely to remain an excited, witnessing Christian.

Fifth, baptism is a summons to forsake sin and the world. It faces the new believer with the need to rely on Christ immediately to begin cleaning up his life. Suppose, for instance, that the new Christian is filled with zeal and yet still displays deep-seated arrogance and a hot temper. This must change, and the preparation for baptism is a good time to get started. I believe that many sins can be uprooted quickly from the new believer's life if they are faced during the early period of "glow" which comes when he sees his sins covered by the blood of Christ.

Furthermore, baptism is a summons not only to separate from the world of sin, but to be ready to suffer its attacks. For a youth from an inner city gang, this can mean his life. William Krispin, an urban home missionary in Philadelphia, says, "In many places in the inner city, baptism is a life and death issue for the teenager. It means that you are separating from a whole way of life for the sake of Christ, and you are putting your life on the line with the gang.'' For the suburbanite, the conflict with the world takes a different form, but it can be vicious in spite of the greater sophistication. Persecution may follow baptism in the form of an abruptly ended friendship, a sneer, a wave of cruel gossip, or a direct verbal attack. Nevertheless, its coming reminds the believer that our baptism sacramentally portrays and seals our union with Christ, and in that union there must be an identification with His suffering. Christ's *atoning* sufferings were completed at Calvary, but our identification with Him includes our suffering at the hands of the world (Matt. 20:22-23; John 12:20-26; Phil. 1:27-30; Col. 1:24). We must teach believers new and old that suffering is our lot from unbelievers. We leaders have not taught our people that their baptism includes this summons, and as a result our people are easily intimidated in witness. They are silenced by the fear of human opinion.

Sixth, an emphasis on prompt baptism of new Christians can influence the life of even the most staid congregation. Older Christians can be stirred to life by the embarrassing freshness and boldness of the new convert. They are challenged to confess their sin of silence and to share the Word with new power. Those who are unconverted are also confronted with the work of God. Some will be led to conversion, increasing the power of the church's testimony. Others may slip out of the fellowship, frightened by the nearness of the living God. Others may persecute anyone closely tied to this new ministry of the Spirit, rightly seeing it as threat to their carnal security, their right to live a life undisturbed by the Word and Spirit.

For church leaders, this visible work of God causes the church service to take on a new relevance and vitality. Of all present, they are most directly confronted with the work of God in the regeneration of new believers. Often they are convicted of their responsibility for the metronomic worship style which has lulled their congregations to sleep. Simple testimonies by new

Christians go a long way toward breaking leaders out of the iron grip of routine and formalism that so readily take over in their lives.

Having said all this, I am sensitive to the objection that, in our Presbyterian and Reformed tradition, adult baptism has only been permitted following a lengthy period of doctrinal instruction. I grant that the tradition is a strong one, but we need to ask what the Scriptures say on these matters.

The Great Commission states: "Go therefore and make disciples of all nations, baptizing them into the name of the Father, and of the Son and of the Holy Spirit, teaching them to observe all things that I have commanded you" (Matt. 28:19-20a, RSV). Note the order stated in the passage: baptism comes first, followed by the fulness of teaching. It is not that teaching is omitted before baptism, but that, prior to baptism, it focuses on salvation and public confession of Christ. The rest is to come afterwards.

The book of Acts powerfully confirms this interpretation of the Great Commission. I would commend to the Christian leader the study of the following passages on baptism in the book of Acts: 2:37-42; 8:12-13, 26-40; 10:44-48; 16:14-15, 31-34; 22:6-16. What exists in all of them is a pattern of speedy, if not immediate, baptism upon conversion.

It might be objected that this emphasis on baptism and public witness could lead to a "rebaptizing" of persons who have already been baptized as infants. In reply I would affirm my conviction that baptism is an ordinance of Christ which is not to be repeated. Therefore I want no part in "rebaptizing" those who have been truly baptized. But is "baptism" in a sacramentarian setting a baptism in the biblical sense of that term? In answering that question, we must study the conception of baptism maintained in the particular denomination which administered the "sacrament." If it turns out that the intention is substantially different from that found in Scripture, then you have reason to question the validity of the "baptism." What it comes down to is that the teaching of baptismal regeneration is seriously in conflict with Scripture. Therefore a session might properly conclude that an "infant baptism" carried out with such an unbiblical intention is no baptism at all, and proceed to the application of this ordinance to the new Christian.

To summarize, baptism is a covenantal sign of the visible passage by which the new Christian enters fully into his new life. His public confession unites him in fellowship with his brethren. He comes to see his place in God's kingdom as part of the people of God, whose common purpose is to witness to the world with praises to the God who called him out of darkness into His marvelous light (I Pet. 2:9). The more this sign and the accompanying confession are given prominence in worship, the greater will be the blessing upon our corporate life and witness.

CHAPTER FOURTEEN

Mobilizing through Faith:
God's Way to Do God's Work

Every attempt to counsel a pastor on mobilizing his congregation for witness (including this one) fills his mind with admonitions and suggestions regarding his task. I would like to end this book with a reminder of what his task is *not:* he has *not* been called to create the mandate for evangelism nor must he provide the spiritual power to carry it out. The Lord of the church is the one who has furnished both the mandate and the means for her global witness. We might say that we do not create Pentecost; Pentecost creates us. We are part of God's new creation, joining with Christ as He extends the spread of new life around the globe. All that is asked of us is that we lay hold of Christ in such a way that our lives are daily transformed to share the mind, power and heart of the Lord Jesus.

In his commentary on John 1:16, Calvin discusses how the fulness of God is available to the believer: ''In Christ the wealth of all these things is laid before us that we may seek them in Him. Of His own will He is ready to flow to us, if only we make way for Him by faith.''[1] Note Calvin's last clause. It is faith alone that lays hold of Christ's fulness for us, at the moment of our conversion and through our Christian life. Without faith, what we have learned of Christ's practical sovereignty will be useless to us. We will lack the power of Christ to undertake our

---

1. John Calvin, *Calvin's Commentaries, The Gospel According to St. John,* trans. T. H. L. Parker (Grand Rapids: William B. Eerdmans Publishing Co., 1959), vol. I, p.23.

ministries. What we need, then, is to understand the nature of faith and how it appropriates Christ's fulness for our lives and witness.

From the moment of our justification, the function of biblical faith is to receive from Christ that which we lack in ourselves. We receive God's salvation when we abandon our own efforts and claim Christ's righteousness as our own by faith in His work for us. Faith is God's gift (Eph. 2:8-10); it is the means He uses to transfer His fulness and life to us. When faith is properly exercised, God bestows on us what once belonged solely to Him—perfect righteousness, the Holy Spirit, the fruits of the Spirit, etc. The windows of heaven are opened wide to the man whose arms are spread out in faith!

Because that is so, the Scriptures go on to affirm that faith can indeed do marvelous things. Perhaps the most astonishing passage on the subject is Mark 9:23b: "All things are possible to him that believeth." Our familiarity with this verse has done much to weaken the impact of its promise, but the words hit us with renewed force when we realize that ultimately it is of God alone that we can say, "All things are possible to *Him*." Men and angels certainly lack that power in themselves, yet God, through Christ, promises *all power* to our faith. What Christ is actually saying is that faith, in its receptive, appropriating character, receives God Himself! It has nothing to do with man's moral achievements or intellectual strivings. Faith is a dependence on Christ's indwelling that Scripture variously describes as "looking," "seeing," "coming," "resting," "receiving," and even "eating" and "drinking."

This amazing truth should help us to see many things more clearly. For one, it should help us understand the missionary failure of so many congregations today. Plainly, God would have us see that all the resources have been available for accomplishing the deeds of God. What has failed is our appropriating faith. The promises of God have gone unclaimed, with no one to embrace them as their own, and the church has more and more retreated into her protective shell.

102

If that is the case, what can we do about it? The cure for this grave sin of unbelief is to get back to the Scriptures as God's missionary epistle setting forth His vision of mercy in Christ. We need to read the Bible in a new way: to claim its promises as the personal commitments of our loving Father, and to receive its directives to the New Testament church as directives to us as well. The result would be a witness of such boldness and commitment that cultists would blush over their comparative lack of zeal!

One more question remains. We have seen that faith is what we need to receive the fulness of God into our lives, but how exactly is this accomplished? It is through prayer that faith reaches out to Christ and His abundance of grace. In this communication with our heavenly Father, our hearts are softened and attuned to the missionary nature of God. Through prayer God brings the severity of the law and the dreadful fate of the lost home to our understanding. He gives us a fresh awareness of the wonder of His gift to the world in Christ. And it is through prayer that the New Testament picture of a vital, witnessing church comes alive. We receive the mind, the heart and power of Jesus Christ.

God uses the prayer of faith to bring the fulness of Christ into our churches and our lives, for when we pray, our faith becomes daring through the power of love. The "faith that works by love" (Gal. 5:6) enables its possessor to fulfill the command to love your neighbor as yourself (5:13-14) and to walk in the Spirit and put to death the works of the flesh (5:16-26). The verb translated "works" in verse 6 has in it the idea of unusual energy, even supernatural power. Clearly, God is eager to perform His works through us. Let us claim, with great anticipation, Paul's prayer as our own: "Finally, brethren, pray for us, that the word of the Lord may speed on and triumph, as it did among you" (II Thess. 3:1, RSV).

Selected Bibliography for Evangelism

Theological and Doctrinal Basis for Evangelism

Allen, Roland. *Missionary Principles*. London: Roxburghe House, 1913.

Bavinck, Herman. *Our Reasonable Faith*. Grand Rapids: Wm. B. Eerdmans Publishing Company, 1956, pp. 386-483.

Bavinck, J.H. *An Introduction to the Science of Missions*. Philadelphia: Presbyterian and Reformed Publishing Company, 1960.

Calvin, John. *Institutes of the Christian Religion*. Grand Rapids: Wm. B. Eerdmans Publishing Company, 1953, Bk.I, Chaps. I-X.

Chantry, Walter. *Today's Gospel: Authentic or Synthetic?* London: Banner of Truth, 1970.

Di Gangi, Mariano. *Evangelism, Enterprise of Love*. Nutley, N.J.: Presbyterian and Reformed Publishing Company, 1973.

Howard, David, editor. *Declare His Glory Among the Nations*. Downers Grove, Illinois: Intervarsity Press, 1977.

Kuiper, R.B. *For Whom Did Christ Die?* Grand Rapids: Wm. B. Eerdmans Publishing Company, 1959.

————. *God-Centered Evangelism: A Presentation of the Scriptural Theology of Evangelism*. London: Banner of Truth, 1961.

Kuyper, Abraham. *The Work of the Holy Spirit*. Grand Rapids: Wm. B. Eerdmans Publishing Company, 1956, pp. 304-21, 338-53.

Monsma, Martin. "The Fundamental Principles of Reformed Evangelism," *Reformed Evangelism*. Grand Rapids: Baker Book House, 1948.

Morgan, G. Campbell. *Evangelism*. London: Henry E. Walter, Ltd., 1964.

Morris, Leon. *The Apostolic Preaching of the Cross*. London: Tyndale Press, 1955.

Murray, John, and Calvin K. Cummings, editors. *Biblical Evangelism Today*. Philadelphia: Committee on Christian Education, Orthodox Presbyterian Church, 1954.

Murray, John, and Ned. B. Stonehouse. "The Free Offer of the Gospel." Phillipsburg, N.J.: Lewis J. Grotenhuis, n.d.

Packer, J.I. *Evangelism and the Sovereignty of God*. Chicago: Intervarsity Press, 1961.

Schaeffer, Francis. *The God Who Is There*. Downers Grove, Ill.: Intervarsity Press, 1968.

Stewart, James A. *New Testament Evangelism*. Chattanooga, Tenn.: Revival Literature, n.d.

Thielicke, Helmut. *Encounter with Spurgeon*. Philadelphia: Fortress Press, 1963.

Van Peursem, William. "Motives and Incentives for Evangelism," *Reformed Evangelism*. Grand Rapids: Baker Book House, 1948.

Vos, Geerhardus. "Repentance and Faith," *The Kingdom and the Church*. Grand Rapids: Wm. B. Eerdmans Publishing Company, 1958.

Watson, David. *I Believe in Evangelism*. Grand Rapids: Eerdmans, 1976.

Wolf, Carl Julius, editor. *Jonathan Edwards on Evangelism*. Grand Rapids: Wm. B. Eerdmans Publishing Company, 1958.

Preparation for Evangelism:

Berg, Johannes van den. *Constrained by Jesus' Love*. Kampen: J. H. Kok, 1956.

Bonar, Horatius. *Words to Winners of Souls*. Oradell, New Jersey: American Tract Society, n.d.

Bridges, Charles. "Causes of Ministerial In-Efficiency Connected with Our Personal Character," *The Christian Ministry*, Part III. London: Banner of Truth, 1967.

Calvin, John. *Institutes of The Christian Religion*. Bk. III, chaps. VI-XI.

Hughes, Philip E. "The Instruments God Uses," *Revive Us Again*. Marshall, Morgan & Scott, 1947.

Owen, John. "The Glory of Christ" *The Works of John Owen*. vol. I. London: Banner of Truth, 1965.

Pink, Arthur. *Profiting from the Word*. London: Banner of Truth Trust, 1970.

Ravenhill, Leonard. *Why Revival Tarries*. Minneapolis: Bethany Fellowship, Inc., 1959.

Sprague, William B. "Obstacles to Revival," *Lectures of Revivals*. London: Banner of Truth, 1959, pp. 61-87.

Stott, John R. *Motives and Method in Evangelism*. London: Intervarsity Press, 1962.

———. *The Preacher's Portrait*. London: Tyndale Press, 1961.

Verwer, George. *A Revolution of Love*. Kansas City, Kansas: Walterick Publishers, n.d.

Personal Evangelism:

Little, Paul. *How to Give Away Your Faith*. Chicago: Intervarsity Press, 1966.

Rinker, Rosalyn, and Harry Griffith. *Sharing God's Love*. Grand Rapids: Zondervan Publishing, 1976.

Sanny, Lorne. *The Art of Personal Witnessing*. Chicago: Moody Press, 1957.

Spurgeon, Charles Haddon. *The Soul Winner* or *How to Lead Sinners to the Savior*. London: Marshall, n.d.

Stott, John R.W. *Personal Evangelism*. London: Intervarsity Press, 1969.

Turnbull, Charles T.G. *Taking Men Alive*. London: Lutterworth Press, 1957.

Approach in Youth Evangelism (including children):

Braund, Elizabeth. "Our Street" I, II, *The Evangelical Magazine* (November-December, 1963; January-February, 1964).

———. "The Tragedy of the Teen-Ager," *The Evangelical Magazine* (May-June, 1963).

———. "The Cross and the Switchblade—and Us,"*The Evangelical Magazine* (November-December, 1965).

Gailliet, Emile. *Young Life*. New York: Harper and Row, 1963.

Greer, Virginia. *Give Them Their Dignity*. Richmond, Va.: John Knox Press, 1968.

Inchley, John. *Kids in the Kingdom*. Wheaton, Ill.: Tyndale House Publishers, 1977.

Murray, Andrew. *The Children for Christ*. London: J. Nisbet, 1887.

Approach to Particular Groups:

Ellison, H.L. *The Christian Approach to the Jew*. London: Edinburgh House, 1958.

Garver, Stuart P. *Watch Your Teaching: A Comparative Study of Roman Catholic and Protestant Teaching Since Vatican Council II*. Hackensack, N.J.: Christ's Mission, Inc. 1973.

Guinness, Os. *Encircling Eyes*. Downers Grove: Intervarsity Press, 1974.

Howard, David. *Student Power in World Evangelism*. Downers Grove, Ill.: Intervarsity Press, 1970.

Miller, C. John. *Witnessing to the American Businessman*. Decatur, Georgia: Presbyterian Evangelistic Fellowship, n.d.

————. *Witnessing to the Dying*. Decatur, Ga.: Presbyterian Evangelistic Fellowship, n.d.

————. *Witnessing to Jevohah Witnesses*. Decatur, Ga.: Presbyterian Evangelistic Fellowship, n.d.

————. *Witnessing to Roman Catholics*. Decatur, Ga.: Presbyterian Evangelistic Fellowship, n.d.

Rosen, Moishe. *How to Witness Simply and Effectively to the Jews*. San Rafel, Calif.: Jews for Jesus, n.d.

Skinner, Tom. *Black and Free*. Grand Rapids: Zondervan Publishing House, 1968.

Programs of Evangelism for the Local Church:

A. *Hospitality and Home Bible Study*

Geiger, Terry. *Friendship Evangelism*. P. O. Box 325, Coral Gables, Fla.: Men in Action, n.d.

Kromminga, Carl. *Bringing God's News to Neighbors*. Nutley, N.J.: Prebyterian and Reformed Publ. Co., 1976.

Mains, Karen. *Open Heart, Open Home*. Elgin, Ill.: D.C. Cook Publishing Co., 1976.

McGavran, Donald A. *How Churches Grow*. New York: Friendship Press, 1966.

————. *The Bridges of God*. New York: Friendship Press, 1955.

Milliken, Bill. *Tough Love*. Old Tappan, N.J.: F.H. Revell Co., 1968

Schaeffer, Edith. *L'Abri*. Wheaton: Tyndale House Publishers, 1969.

Wollen, Albert. *How to Conduct Home Bible Classes*. Wheaton, Ill.: Scripture Press, 1969.

————. *Miracles Happen in Small Group Bible Study*. Glendale: Gospel Light Press, 1976.

B. *Mobilizing for Witness*.

Autrey, C.E. *Basic Evangelism*. Grand Rapids: Zondervan Publishing House, 1959.

Baxter, Richard. "Directions for the Right Managing of this Work," *The Reformed Pastor*. New York: Robert Carter, 1860.

Hodges, Melvin L. "Creating Climate for Church Growth," *Church Growth and Christian Mission,* ed. Donald A. McGavran. New York: Harper and Row Publishers, 1965.

Kennedy, D. James. *Evangelism Explosion*. Wheaton, Ill.: Tyndale House Press, 1970.

Stott, John R.W. *Our Guilty Silence*. London: Hodder and Stoughton, 1967.

Sharing the Missionary Vision with the Local Church:

Allen, Roland. *Missionary Methods: St. Paul's or Ours?* London: Robert Scott, 1912.

Blauw, Johannes. *The Missionary Nature of the Church*. New York: McGraw Hill, 1962.

Boer, Harry. *Pentecost and Missions*. Grand Rapids: Wm. B. Eerdmans, 1961.

Carey, William. *An Enquiry into the Obligations of Christians to Use Means for the Conversion of the Heathens*. London: The Carey Kingsgate Press, 1961.

De Ridder, Richard. *Discipling the Nations*. Grand Rapids: Baker Book House, 1975.

Jeremias, Joachim. *Jesus' Promise to the Nations*. London: SCM Press Ltd., 1958.

Nevius, John L. *The Planting and Development of Missionary Churches*. Grand Rapids: Baker Book House, 1958.

Rowley, H.H. *The Missionary Message of the Old Testament*. London: Carey Press, 1944.

Shepherd, Walter D. *Sent by the Sovereign*. Nutley, N.J.: Presbyterian and Reformed Publishing Company, 1968.

Stott, John R.W. *Christian Mission in the Modern World*. Downers Grove, Ill.: Intervarsity Press, 1975.

Planning and Training for Evangelism in the Local Church:

Alexander, Archibald. *Log College*. London: Banner of Truth, 1968.

Braun, Niel. *Laity Mobilized: Reflections on Church Growth in Japan and Other Lands*. Grand Rapids: Wm. B. Eerdmans Publishing Company, 1971.

Bruce, A.B. *The Training of the Twelve*, 4th ed., rev. Hodder & Stoughton, n.d.

Coleman, Robert E. *The Master Plan of Evangelism*. Westwood, N.J.: Fleming H. Revell Co., 1963.

Fish, R.J. *Study Guide to the Master Plan of Evangelism*. Old Tappan, N.J.: Fleming Revell Co., 1972.

Green, Michael. "Evangelistic Methods," *Evangelism in the Early Church*. Grand Rapids: Wm. B. Eerdmans Publishing Co., 1970.

Greenway, Roger S. *Calling Our Cities to Christ*. Nutley, N.J.: Presbyterian and Reformed Publishing Company, 1973.

———. *An Urban Strategy for Latin America*. Grand Rapids: Baker Book House, 1973.

Kennedy, D. James. *Evangelism Explosion*. Wheaton: Tyndale House, 1970.

Kuhne, Gary. *The Dynamics of Personal Follow-Up*. Grand Rapids: Zondervan Publishing House, 1976.

Moore, Waylon B. *New Testament Follow-Up*. Grand Rapids: Wm. B. Eerdmans Publishing Company, 1975.

Oldham, J.H. *Florence Allshorn and the Story of St. Julians*. New York: Harper and Row Publishers, n.d.

Richardson, Don. *Peace Child*. Glendale, Calif.: Gospel Light, 1974.

Taylor, Mrs. Howard. *Behind the Ranges*. London: Lutterworth Press and the China Inland Mission, 1944.

Prayer and Evangelism in the Local Church:

Bounds, E.M. *Power Through Prayer*. Grand Rapids: Baker Book House, 1963.

Bruce, A.B. "Lessons in Prayer," *The Training of the Twelve,* 4th ed., rev. Hodder and Stoughton, n.d.

Calvin, John. *Institutes of the Christian Religion*. Book III. Philadelphia: Presbyterian Board of Christian Education, 1939.

Conn, Harvie M. "Luke's Theology of Prayer," *Christianity Today* XVII, 6 (December 22, 1972), 290-92.

Hallesby, O.A. *Prayer,* translated by Clarence J. Carlsen, Minneapolis: Augsburg Press, 1937.

Murray, Andrew. *With Christ in the School of Prayer*. Old Tappan, N.J.: Fleming H. Revell.

Orr, J. Edwin. *The Fervent Prayer: The Worldwide Impact of the Great Awakening of 1858*. Chicago: Moody Press, 1974

Phelps, Austin. *The Still Hour,* or *Communion with God*. Edinburgh: Banner of Truth, reprint.

APPENDIX

A New Life

Have you ever felt there was something missing in your life? Something important but you didn't know what? That may be the **new life** God wants you to have. A life of joy, peace, and fulfillment. A life. . .which you can receive today. Carefully consider these **Five Important Facts** . . . And find out how you can get that new life and become a brand new person.

1. A loving God sent His Son Jesus into the world to bring you a new and abundant life.

Jesus said: "If anyone thirsts, let him come to me and drink. He that believes in me . . . from within him shall flow rivers of living water" (John 7:38-39).

He also said: concerning those He loves: "I came that they might have life and have it abundantly" (John 10:10).

This new life brings you the fruit of the Spirit: "love, joy, peace, patience, kindness, goodness, faithfulness, gentleness, self-control" (Gal. 5:22). **It also gives POWER!**

God's Holy Spirit gives you the power to overcome. . .

Feelings of loneliness, stress, fear of people and the future (I John 4:18)

And the power to break unbreakable habits like. . .

selfishness, depression, uncontrolled anger, prejudice, sexual lust, overeating, overdrinking, drug abuse (I Cor. 6:9-11).

But why are so many people without this new life?

2. Because . . . people are self-centered, not God-centered.

This means that by nature you are spiritually dead and deceived. (Ephesians 2:1: "You were dead through your trespasses and sins.")

TO BE SPIRITUALLY DEAD AND DECEIVED is to be centered on yourself and not on your Creator and to believe

A Big Lie

People show this according to Romans 1:21-31 by being . . .

> Unthankful to God, perverted, greedy, jealous,
> bitter, proud, mean, devious, foolish

Since man's first sin, he has tried to be INDEPENDENT of God. Actually each human being is entirely DEPENDENT on God for breath, food, health, shelter, physical and mental abilities. THE BIG LIE: SELFISH INDEPENDENCE:

> self-trust, self-boasting, self-reliance, self-analysis,
> self-hating, self-seeking

3. Self-centered man is separated from a Holy God by three big barriers.

Bad Record
Romans 3:23
"All have sinned. . . ."

Bad Heart
Mark 7:21
"From the heart of man come evil thoughts. . . ."

Bad Master
John 8:34
"Whoever commits sin is a slave. . . ."

Consequences of sin as separation from God. . .
"The wages of sin is death" (Romans 6:23a).
Now

1. A dry, thirsty, unsatisfied life

2. A guilty, accusing conscience
   (depression, fears, etc.)
3. An aging body that must shortly die.

To Come

1. Loss of all friendship and earthly joys forever
   (Matthew 8:12)
2. Frightful pains of body and conscience forever
   (Mark 9:48)
3. Dreadful thirst of soul and body forever
   (Luke 16:19-31)

4. God's Solution! No Barriers!

Perfect Record
I Corinthians 1:30
"Christ . . . is made our righteousness."

New Heart
Ezekiel 36:25-26
"A new heart I will give you."

Good Master
Matthew 11:28-30
"My yoke is easy."

"The blood of Jesus, God's Son, cleanses us from all sin" (I John 1:7).

The benefit of Jesus' death . . . Love's Biggest Gift
"The free gift of God is eternal life through Jesus Christ" (Romans 6:23). Jesus the God-man is the biggest gift of the Father's love. On the cross Jesus suffered all the torments of hell as a substitute for His people (John 3:16, 10:15). He was legally condemned by God as their representative, removing the barriers of a bad record, a bad heart, and a bad master. The Father's love can do no more. Risen from the dead, Jesus now lives to give you a new record, a new heart, Himself as new master— and the free gift of eternal life now!

You Need to Make Sure:

> God says you either have a NEW LIFE or you are a
> lawbreaker DEAD in your self-centeredness. Are you per-
> sonally alive or dead? If you are still dead, you need to
> know . . .

5. How to receive the Lord Jesus into your life . . .

1. Turn

> in sorrow from your sins: "Let the wicked forsake his
> way, and the unrighteous man his thoughts; let him turn
> to the Lord, that He may have mercy on him, and to our
> God, for He will abundantly pardon" (Isaiah 55:7).

2. Trust

> in Christ Jesus alone: "Believe in the Lord Jesus Christ
> and thou shalt be saved, and thy house" (Acts 16:31).

Repentance is . . . not our suffering or our good works to earn
our salvation, but a turning from our sins to the living God
through Jesus Christ.

Trust in the Lord Jesus is . . . accepting, receiving, and resting on Him alone as the Savior from our sins.

Begin A NEW LIFE

Will you now surrender your life to Christ by turning from your
self-centered way and trusting in Him alone?

Here is a guideline to help you confess your sins and come to
know God through taking the Lord Jesus Christ as your *own*
personal Savior:

"Heavenly Father, I am really a selfish person. I have wanted my own way—not
yours. I have often been jealous, proud, and rebellious. You are my Creator, but
I have acted as though I was lord of all. I have not been thankful to you. I have
not listened to your Word the Bible and have not loved your Son. But now I see
that all my sin is against you. I now repent of this evil attitude. I turn from all my

116

sins and trust that Jesus shed His precious blood to cleanse me from all my guilt. I now receive Him as my Savior and the Lord of my life."

I, _____, turn from my sins and take Christ as my Lord and Savior. By His help I promise to obey Him in every part of my life.

How Does This New Life Continue?

The same way it began—in faith and prayer.

1. Pray constantly. . .   Prayer is talking to God. Keep doing it all the time. Include in it praise, thanksgiving, confession of sins, petitions for others salvation, and requests for help.

2. Read your Bible. . .   Study your Bible every day. It is the food for your new life and your sure guide. In it you meet Jesus and learn to claim His promises for your life.

3. Worship with others. . .Meet with a church where the Bible is taught and obeyed and where Jesus Christ is Lord and Savior.

4. Witness to others. . .   Tell your friends what Christ has done for you—and wants to do for them. Be tactful and back up your words by improvement in manners and doing deeds of kindness.

This booklet has been designed to introduce you to Jesus Christ the author of eternal life. If it has been helpful to you and you have questions or comments contact C. John Miller, 415 Walnut Street, Jenkintown, Pa. 19046; Phone 215/887-5327.

Additional copies of this booklet for sharing Christ with others are available at 10 cents each. Contact P.E.F., Box 1890, Decatur, Georgia 30031. Phone 404/244-0740.